Party Animals

Reviews of Olivia O'Leary's bestselling companion volume,
Politicians and Other Animals:

'Perfect bedside reading for the political junkie …
acerbic, witty, moving, angry and irreverent.'
Rosita Boland, *The Irish Times*

'A great recovery read for political animals.'
Ivana Bacik, *The Irish Times*

'Plenty to stir the interests of the politically aware.'
Fergus Finlay, *Irish Examiner*

Olivia O'Leary was educated at St Leo's College, Carlow and University College Dublin, and trained as a journalist with the *Carlow Nationalist*. Her career as a current-affairs presenter began in 1972 with RTÉ. In the late seventies and early eighties, she moved back to print journalism with *The Irish Times*. The eighties also saw her presenting RTÉ's 'Questions and Answers', 'Today Tonight', later 'Prime Time', and BBC's 'Newsnight'. She continued to further her newspaper links with the *Sunday Tribune* in 1994. She has won three Jacob's Awards, two for television, and one for radio, and the BBC Radio 4 programme 'Between Ourselves' won a Sony Award. Her political musings regularly come to us from 'Five-Seven Live' on RTÉ radio.

Party Animals is a companion volume to Olivia O'Leary's hugely successful *Politicians and Other Animals*.

OLIVIA O'LEARY

PARTY ANIMALS

THE O'BRIEN PRESS
DUBLIN

PUBLISHED IN ASSOCIATION WITH RTÉ

First published 2006 by The O'Brien Press Ltd,
12 Terenure Road East, Dublin 6, Ireland.
Tel: +353 1 4923333; Fax: +353 1 4922777
E-mail: books@obrien.ie
Website: www.obrien.ie
Reprinted 2006, 2007.

ISBN: 978-0-86278-970-1

British Library Cataloguing-in-Publication Data
O'Leary, Olivia, 1949-
Party animals
1. Politicians - Ireland - Anecdotes 2. Ireland - Politics
and government - 21st century 3. Ireland - Social
conditions - 21st century
I. Title
941.7'0824

3 4 5 6 7
07 08 09 10

Cover illustrations: Martyn Turner
Editing, typesetting, layout and design: The O'Brien Press Ltd
Printing: Cox and Wyman Ltd

For Paul and Emily

Acknowledgements

To the politicians, press officers, civil servants and academics who are decent enough to talk to me freely, I say thanks in the best way I possibly can: I won't mention their names. Many thanks, too, to the journalistic colleagues who shared their knowledge and experience with me. They are absolved from all blame for what appears under my name.

I am particularly grateful to the staff of the RTÉ library, of *The Irish Times* library and of the Dún Laoghaire-Rathdown County Council libraries. Time and again they helped me above and beyond the call of duty. Thanks to Paul Durcan for allowing me to quote his poem 'The Hay Carrier' from *A Snail in My Prime*, the Harvill Press, 1993. Thanks, too, to Niall O'Flynn, series producer of 'Five-Seven Live' and his successor, Conor Kavanagh, and to presenters Rachael English and Philip Boucher-Hayes for their encouragement and help; to all at O'Brien Press including my hard-working editor Susan Houlden and designer Emma Byrne; and a very big thank you to Martyn Turner for his inimitable drawings. Lastly, thanks to family and friends whose best lines and memories I have shamelessly stolen and recycled; and to Paul and Emily who make it all worthwhile.

Contents

INTRODUCTION

It was May 1978. Garret FitzGerald looked up to where
his hand was waving, all by itself as it were, to the cheer-
ing Ard-Fheis crowd. He wanted to disown the hand –
you knew that by the smile of acute embarrassment on
his face – but the Fine Gael handlers had insisted that
their new and popular leader must wave to his adoring
public. FitzGerald hated it.

He hated the deification of the leader, hated being carried shoulder high through unthinking, enthusiastic supporters, hated being an object of admiration whose form
he couldn't always dictate. But he did it because he knew
this was the price a man of ideas had to pay for power.
By the late 1970s, the era of the presidential leader had
begun. For thirty years it has shaped the way party politics is conducted in this country. If this book is largely
about party leaders, that's why.

Blame some of it on Séamus Brennan. As a young
Fianna Fáil general secretary, he was charged with helping to ensure that Jack Lynch won the 1977 election. So
he spent two months with the Democratic campaign in

the US to pick up some tips from the 1976 Carter *v* Ford Presidential race. What he saw was the future style Irish electioneering must take, shaped for an age of television and consumerism.

He came back with plans for giant posters, campaign battlebuses, TV ads. He persuaded Jack Lynch to challenge Liam Cosgrave to a TV election debate. Cosgrave refused, saying it was a gimmick, but Fianna Fáil got all the right headlines. Singer Colm Wilkinson recorded an election song, 'Your Kind of Country'. It was banned after a week by RTÉ, one way of ensuring that everyone wanted to hear it. The same slogan appeared on thousands of party t-shirts. Everyone wanted one – it was hot that summer. An exasperated Des O'Malley rang Brennan from Limerick asking: 'Has the whole place gone mad? There's a crowd of nuns out here looking for forty t-shirts!'

Election songs, party hats, balloons – these were all the tricks used by advertisers to sell a commercial product – in this case, the candidate. For this sort of mass publicity campaign in a television age, most policy messages were too complicated, too confusing. You needed a single product with easy brand recognition. It was simple. You marketed the leader.

If, that was, you had a leader who was marketable. Jack Lynch was fine. He was already a sporting hero, and likely to appeal to a wide electorate including the large number of youngsters voting in 1977 when the voting age was lowered to eighteen. Lynch also suited an age which was moving away from megaphones and chapel-gate meetings. Ireland's public debate now happened on the national television service which had expanded and moved from black and white to colour, and people had got used to the shorter, feel-good messages of commercial advertising. Lynch's avuncular, pipe-smoking presence suited the more intimate atmosphere of a television studio. People watching from their armchairs at home felt reassured.

The same couldn't be said for his political rival and Taoiseach since 1973, Liam Cosgrave. On the hustings, there was no better man to belt out a rousing speech, to call up the tribal loyalties. But Cosgrave's bristly moustache and his stiff military bearing looked out of place on television. He was uneasy with the informal style of television interviewing and refused to allow any intrusion into his private life. He avoided the limelight as much as he could and let the many stars in his cabinet shine instead. He belonged to another age.

Cosgrave was the last of the non-presidential leaders. Since then, politics has been all about selling the leader, with slogans like 'Bring Back Jack', 'Let Garret Lead the Way', 'Dessie Can Do It' and 'Arise and follow Charlie' – and the lines that Young Fine Gael are already using to sell Enda Kenny give a foretaste of the next election: t-shirts saying 'I'm with Enda', and banners claiming somewhat blasphemously, 'In Enda we Trust'.

On Charlie Haughey's election campaigns, they used to give out bottles of 'Charlie' perfume. They're a bit more sophisticated nowadays but the tracking of the leaders' popularity ratings is as important in political polling now as is the position of the parties. Party fortunes depend on the leaders, and when they lose elections they're dropped – look at the serial regicide in Fine Gael and the Tory Party. When they win, as our Bert knows, they survive.

And these days they have to fight for every vote. Tribal loyalties are fading fast and people don't vote party so much any more. There's much less 'inertia selling' when competition breaks down the old loyalties, as the Irish banks have now discovered. Political leaders have to trawl for every transfer, from every quarter. Fianna Fáil TDs who instructed their supporters for years to vote only the party ticket, are now writing to known Fine Gael voters, asking humbly to be considered for a second or third preference. Times have changed.

In this tough market, the leader has to have the widest possible appeal and the simplest message. As Fine Gael's canny Strategy Review Group report pointed out in 2003, 'those parties who add the largest proportion of the least politically conscious to their already traditional vote, win elections.' On the mass media, leaders compete with every other product and every other voice. Increasingly, party handlers are pushing the leaders away from harder-edged current affairs programmes and on to entertainment and chat-shows. Here they try to set up a rapport with viewers, talking about their hobbies, their childhood memories, their personal lives – in other words selling themselves and, in the process, the party – reinforcing the brand.

The selling goes on all the time, during and in between elections, and image is everything. There's an increasing concentration on presentation, on clothes, on make-up for television (and not a bald man in sight because it's true, as Hillary Clinton once told Yale students: hair matters in politics). Bertie's had an elocution teacher working on his 'th's'– not too much, just enough to keep middle-class voters from wincing; Enda Kenny has been tutored to sound more decisive – not less nice, just more decisive.

Of course, there's a price to be paid for a presidential system where all the power and attention goes to the party leader, where the leader dominates the media and the coverage of parliament. Increasingly, ordinary back-benchers find themselves dealt out of the game. Squeezed out of local government by the ending of the dual mandate, the abolition of the health boards, they find that their role in parliament has been reduced and bypassed by the Partnership Process, and that the presidential leader system leaves them little chance to make their mark. They have to fall in behind the brand. The only muscle they have is their power to change the leader and they flex it every so often as a reminder, particularly when they judge that the leader's performance is putting their seats in danger.

All they can hope now is that the leader has got it right, as they burrow down in their constituencies and focus on the election. For the rest of us, it will all boil down to a choice between two men as head of government, and it's a measure of how far Enda Kenny has come in four years that there is a genuine choice: Bertie or Enda, who do we trust?

Politicians live from one election to the next and the pieces in this book and its companion volume, *Politicians and Other Animals*, do the same, covering a period between the general election of 2002 and the forthcoming election of 2007. They are mainly, but not all political. They track the rise and fall in party fortunes, in individual careers, but most of all they look at leaders – past, present and future. What do we know about them? What shaped them? Can we trust them?

Read on.

CHARLIE

The Man who Failed Himself

He didn't believe in himself. That's the irony. Despite all the swagger and the swashbuckling, he didn't believe in himself. He had all the gifts. He would have risen to the top in almost any chosen career. All he had to do was play it straight. But deep down, he must have felt he wasn't really good enough.

Why else would a man so talented, so well-educated and well-connected, have resorted to the cheap political strokes, the bands of yes-men? Why else would he have needed to ape the belted earls his own party dismissed so contemptuously? Did he feel he was nothing without the mansion, the island, the yacht? For a man as bright as he was, it was sad.

He surrounded himself with courtiers – loyalty was the only requirement. The veteran *Irish Times* political editor, Dick Walsh, remembers seeing him during one of those turbulent Fianna Fáil Ard-Fheiseanna in the early 1970s. Haughey, then exiled to the backbenches, walked across the road to one of the pubs opposite the RDS, flanked by the usual band of supporters. Needing to make a phone-call, he went to the coin-box. As Haughey held the handpiece, one courtier dropped in the money for him, another dialled the number. He accepted such slavish attention as though born to it.

Like that other well-known man of the people, François Mitterand, he developed the princely manner. Only Mitterand had the same imperious side-sweep of the hand which indicated dismissal from his presence. Only Mitterand wore the trappings of office with quite the same air of divine right.

He was fascinated by the Medici and saw himself in the mould of Lorenzo il Magnifico – leader of the Florentine Republic, wily politician, great patron of the arts, the man who typified the spirit of the Renaissance. Haughey loved to hear stories about the Medici from his friend, the art curator and commentator, Ciarán MacGonigal, who had lived and studied in Florence. There was one in particular about Lorenzo surviving an attempted coup. The powerful Pazzi family had arranged to kill Lorenzo and his brother Giuliano during Easter Mass at the Duomo. At the elevation of the host, when everybody knelt down and lowered their heads, the assassins attacked. But Lorenzo, who had not lowered his head, escaped to the sacristy. Barricaded in there, he sent for help and soon the entire Pazzi family was done away with, including Archbishop Salviati who was hung from a window in the Palazzo Vecchio. Survivor of numerous coups himself, Haughey identified with that one. 'Tell me that story again,' he'd beg Ciarán.

Great figures who combined statesmanship and patronage of the arts impressed him particularly, so Louis XIV and Louis XV were heroes. Talking to MacGonigal one day about the business of nurturing a successor, he asked what the Bourbons had said on the subject. MacGonigal quoted to him the great declaration of Louis XV: 'Après moi le deluge.' 'Yes, that'll do for me,' said Charlie happily.

He rarely missed a chance for a put-down. He gave me a lift back to Dublin in his blue Mercedes during one of the election campaigns. He sat silently in front perusing papers. I sat in the back chatting to PJ Mara. I made some joke about vintage Lynch-Bages wine and mispronounced it in the process. I can still remember how Haughey turned right around to bestow on me his look of coldest contempt.

He would arrive early for interviews, totally wrong-footing the interviewer. Abandoning make-up and dragging a brush through my hair, I would race into studio to find him already seated and drumming his fingers. To any small talk, he would respond only with a haughty nod, or a silent shake of the head.

That was when he was in power. During an election, however, where he needed to please, he used charm. With women interviewers – and he knew it always worked – he'd enquire about your children. He always remembered whether they were boys or girls. He always remembered their names. I told him once that as a toddler, my daughter would see me on television and want to talk to me. When I didn't respond, she'd get more and more frustrated and start to hit the screen. 'I know,' he murmured. 'I often react to you like that myself.'

He was bright and he knew it. I remember once needing to check the name of the Roman general who abandoned his plough to save Rome from invasion and returned to his farm immediately afterwards, refusing all honours. So I rang the Fianna Fáil rooms looking for my old UCD tutor in Roman History, John Wilson. A gravelly voice answered and asked, 'What d'you want *him* for?' I explained about the Roman general. 'Ah sure what would *he* know about it?' said the gravelly voice. '*I'll* tell you. It was Cincinnatus.' Haughey always enjoyed knowing more than everyone else.

He was a gift to newspaper editors. Just like a Princess Diana front page would add massively to the sale of any newspaper or magazine, the same held true for Haughey in Ireland. Put Haughey or Gay Byrne on the front page and the circulation went up. People were fascinated by him – they loved or hated him in equal measure – but they were endlessly curious about him. He created controversy and he thrived on division. In opposition, he opposed for the sake of opposing, whether it was the Anglo-Irish Agreement, or the long-overdue liberalisation of the family planning laws he had himself introduced. In government, where he could, he sidelined those who hadn't supported him for the leadership.

He settled scores in other areas too. I didn't like him much. It was mutual and I was presenting 'Questions and Answers' when he came into power in 1987. Suddenly, I found that no cabinet ministers were available to come on the programme. In despair one Friday, I by-passed PJ Mara and the press office and rang a minister myself – Michael O'Kennedy, who was Minister for Foreign Affairs. O'Kennedy immediately agreed to come on. Next day, the programme researcher got an irate and rude phone-call from Mara, saying that O'Kennedy would now not be coming on and warning us never again to by-pass the press office. There would be no government ministers.

He understood television better than any politician I've dealt with other than Tony Blair. He might have a temper tantrum off-camera, but never on. He never let himself get riled by the interviewer. He always saw past the interviewer to the voter watching at home. So he gave calm, reasonable answers in simple language. He never brought notes into the studio. Garret FitzGerald always had sheaves of paper, but Haughey knew instinctively that looking down at papers would make him appear distracted. It also meant that he presented a balding pate to the camera when what people needed to see were his eyes. Rightly or wrongly, they trust you more if they see your eyes. He handled the medium so well that it always surprised me he didn't use it more. Instead he was so suspicious of journalists that he limited his appearances to the big occasions. Once again, his own insecurity hobbled him.

He remained wary of the media after he retired, particularly after his appearance at the tribunals. I interviewed him around that time for a television documentary on the then SDLP leader, John Hume. Haughey greeted us courteously at the door of Abbeville and ushered us into the beautiful ballroom. Just as we were about to turn on the camera and start the interview, he turned around and waved a hand at the pale green walls covered with gilt-edged paintings. 'You won't be including all this in the picture, will you?' 'Why?' I asked innocently.' Are you worried about burglars?' 'No,' he said, eyes narrowing. 'I just don't want references to gilded lifestyles – less of the gilded lifestyle, OK?'

He was insecure about the portraits painted of him as Taoiseach as well. About half a dozen were produced and languished in the bowels of the Board of Works before the portrait by John F Kelly which now hangs in the Dáil.

He was a bad loser. When his candidate, Brian Lenihan, lost the presidential election, he spent the next year trying to clip the wings of the woman who won, Mary Robinson. As Helen Burke and I described it in *Mary Robinson – the authorised biography*, invitations to President Robinson to open conferences or new enterprises would suddenly be withdrawn. Difficulties would be put in the way of the organisers. One example was an invitation to open the conference of 'Women into Technology in the European Community' in connection with NETWORK, the Irishwomen's business organisation. The invitation was withdrawn when the organisers were told that they would lose the venue unless a government minister performed the opening.

Robinson was getting international recognition and that was galling for a Taoiseach who had enjoyed striding the international stage with Ireland's Presidency of the European Union the previous year. He tried to stop her doing interviews on the basis that they were 'not appropriate'. He stopped her accepting BBC Television's invitation to deliver their annual David Dimpleby lecture. He came to the Áras armed with his senior counsel's opinion that the government had a constitutional veto over any interview or speech she might want to give. Mary Robinson, who was herself a constitutional lawyer, gave battle and Haughey never returned to the fray.

But it was the row over President Robinson's St Patrick's Day message which indicates how deeply he resented the attention she attracted. Bord Fáilte asked the President to record a message as part of a promotional package done by World Television Network to be broadcast across the US on our national day. There was a very good reaction to the broadcast and congratulatory reports came back to the Department of Foreign Affairs and eventually found their way to the Taoiseach's office.

The Taoiseach got upset and the late Martin Dully, then head of Bord Fáilte, was called to Haughey's office where he was met at the door by PJ Mara, warning him that the Boss was in terrible form and that he was going to be bawled out.

Haughey told Dully Bord Fáilte had no right to approach the President directly for anything. 'What could I do,' said Dully, 'but try not to apologise for what all the evidence showed had been a successful campaign? His language was unparliamentary but then that was no different from his language in certain other crises. That was his style.'

There were other examples of temper tantrums, one in particular from about the same period. It showed how he became more and more paranoid as he struggled to hang on to power. Ciarán MacGonigal, then curator of the Grafton Gallery, who had been appointed to the National Gallery by Haughey, was in Claremorris, giving a talk as part of a weekend celebrating the writer George Moore. It was in the months after Haughey had been challenged by Albert Reynolds and Pádraig Flynn and they had both left cabinet. Reynolds and Flynn were interested in pushing an arts scholarship scheme for the area and asked MacGonigal, as an expert on the arts, to talk to them about it. They chatted for nearly two hours in the hotel lobby. When MacGonigal returned home on Sunday evening, there was a message on his answerphone from Haughey. Usually the messages were chatty because, after all, they were friends. This one, says MacGonigal, was ominously formal: 'Mr Haughey wants to see you in his office.'

Early on Monday morning, says MacGonigal, he arrived at the Taoiseach's office. 'He started screaming at me from the door: "F***ing c***ing traitor. F***ing, c***ing traitor." I thought, what have I done? He was screaming, running around the room, throwing files, kicking the tables and chairs. He was turning purple in front of me and I couldn't understand what he was saying except that I had betrayed him and was consorting with his enemies.

'Eventually the decibel level dropped and he said I had been advising somebody who was an enemy of his. When I tried to explain the conversation I had had with Reynolds and Flynn, he said: "So you admit it?" Then he went on about how we were all betraying him and he said he wanted me off the board of the National Gallery. "I made you and I can break you," he said.

'I said he could dismiss me by sending me a letter dismissing me. No, he said, because then it would all be in the papers. I agreed that indeed it would. Then he shouted at me: "I'll destroy your career." He went on about my brother being a Blueshirt (Ciarán's brother Muiris had been Government Press Secretary to the Cosgrave Administration in the seventies). Then he said, "Get out." As I left his office, it was in chaos. There was nobody in the outer office, or in the corridor outside. It was like the *Marie Celeste*.'

The analogy was apt, because even though MacGonigal didn't know it, the ship of state was indeed being abandoned. Haughey would fight to the end to hang on to power but already he was in his last weeks as Taoiseach. The revelation that Haughey knew about Seán Doherty's phone-tapping would bring Haughey down and put Albert Reynolds in as Taoiseach. That day, as MacGonigal crossed the 'Bridge of Sighs', the glass corridor which links the Ministerial Dáil offices to the Dáil, he bumped into Reynolds and Flynn. They said they'd heard he'd been through the wars. They said it would all be over soon and that they would look after him. MacGonigal just wanted to get out of there. He was badly shaken, he said, by the scene he'd been subjected to. He was astounded by the lack of trust from a man he regarded as his friend.

Throughout his career, Haughey's paranoia, his expectation of blind loyalty from his friends, his determination to revenge every slight, constantly sidetracked him and took his focus away from the bigger picture. I was always struck by how easily he let his short-term needs undermine his long-term strategy. Sometimes in a fit of pique, he would throw away a thought-out position. For instance, he must have known that if he really wanted to make progress in Northern Ireland, he needed to have both the British and US governments on board.

That was bound to take time and long-term planning. Yet, he gave up very quickly on the British and on

Thatcher. After two years, he abandoned the tea-pot relationship with her by breaking with EU sanctions against Argentina after the UK sinking of the *Belgrano*. The British were furious but it was manna to the Argentine military junta. I was in Buenos Aires at the time and I woke up one morning to find every radio and television station screaming one name at me: Senor Paddy Power. Every news bulletin led with the news that Ireland had broken with sanctions and reported, 'El Ministro de las Fuerzas Armadas de Irlanda, Senor Paddy Power' as saying that Britain should get out of the Falklands and out of our island too.

Ireland was flavour of the month. Irish Distillers confirmed that sales of Power's whiskey in Argentina suddenly skyrocketed. The very next day I was granted a scoop interview for *The Irish Times* with the Argentine Chancellor, Nicanor Costa Mendes. Haughey's bit of grandstanding, aimed at Fianna Fáil's irredentist heartlands, had made us best buddies with one of the most repressive military governments in the whole world, responsible for torturing and murdering thousands of people. It did us irreparable harm with the UK (Thatcher refused ever to meet Haughey again except on the margins of EU summits) and was no help to us in the US.

He also alienated Ireland's powerful friends in the United States. Ted Kennedy, Daniel Moynihan, Tip O'Neill and Governor Hugh Carey were angered by Haughey's attempts, at the urging of Neil Blaney, to remove Seán Donlon as ambassador to Washington. Donlon, with Jack Lynch's blessing, had waged a successful campaign to move Irish-American opinion away from the Republican fund-raisers, Noraid, and towards the support of constitutional politics in Ireland. Donlon was right morally and strategically in terms of winning US government and political support, and in recognising that the rising generation of rich and respectable Irish-Americans wanted nothing to do with violence. To try to punish him for doing his job was petty and short-sighted, and in the end, Haughey had to back off.

When Garret FitzGerald negotiated the Anglo-Irish Agreement which for the first time gave the Irish government a consultative role in the affairs of Northern Ireland, Haughey denounced it, sending Brian Lenihan to the US to lobby leading politicians against it and once again alienating influential Irish-American supporters. The concession made by the agreement was small, but it was historic, and it was ungenerous of Haughey not to welcome it. Mary Harney broke ranks with Fianna Fáil to vote for it. And, after all his bluster, Haughey once in government did a quiet U-turn and worked easily with the agreement.

In terms of the present peace process, he is widely credited with allowing early contacts with the Republican movement – not greatly credited by the Republican movement, however. In an interview in 1997, Gerry Adams told me pointedly that the Republican movement had approached Haughey early on and that 'Charlie

Haughey spent a long time prevaricating on the issue. He did eventually authorise a meeting between some of us and some senior members of the Fianna Fáil executive and that was a good meeting and was important in building. But it took an Albert Reynolds to actually grasp the nettle.'

There was another job to be done to prepare for peace and reconciliation with Northern Ireland. That was the task of making the Republic a place in which people of all creeds, including Northern Protestants, would not be forced to live by Catholic rules. It was obvious from the seventies that Ireland's laws banning contraception and divorce and criminalising homosexuality would have to be changed – Europe would eventually demand it. But as Minister for Health, Haughey introduced in 1979 the most restrictive family planning legislation possible, which required that a married couple produce a marriage certificate in order to procure contraception. Then, seven years later as opposition leader, he objected to the liberalisation of the law by Minister Barry Desmond. Des O'Malley supported the liberalisation, thereby ending his career in Fianna Fáil, and as he put it in his famous 'I stand by the Republic' speech: 'The politics of this would be very easy. The politics would be to be one of the lads, the safest way in Ireland. But I do not believe that the interests of this State, of our constitution and of this Republic would be served by putting politics before conscience in regard to this.' Haughey remained one of the lads, and while he claimed that Fianna Fáil remained neutral in the 1986 divorce referendum, it was clear that the party quietly campaigned against it.

There are two major achievements, however, for which he will be remembered and rightly so. Firstly, in 1987, he finally found the courage of his convictions and did what he said he would do in January 1980: he tackled our perilous fiscal position. Alan Dukes' decision to support the government in righting our finances made it possible for Haughey to act decisively. Before that, he had often been curiously indecisive, as he was in '80 to '81 when he allowed government finances to swing perilously out of control. A desperate need back then to win his first election as Fianna Fáil leader probably stopped him making the necessary cutbacks. There was no such hesitation in 1987 and his action restored faith in the Irish economy. On this is based our present prosperity. For this we owe him, and Dukes, a large thank you.

Secondly, he had a genuine respect for artists, and that was reflected in the tax exemptions he organised for them as Minister for Finance and in the priority he gave the arts later as Taoiseach. He recognised them publicly through the creation of Aosdána. He created space for them.

He also appreciated the work of the National Museum and ensured the museum services were better funded. The building of the National Concert Hall, the restoration of the Royal Hospital in Kilmainham, the securing of the

Customs House in Limerick as the home of the Hunt Museum – Haughey's hand was to be seen in all those projects.

In this, as in many other ways, he saw himself as a Renaissance Prince. The problem was he expected others to support him in a princely lifestyle – except that this is a Republic and it is as a citizen of a Republic that he failed. He didn't pay his taxes; he initially lied to a public tribunal; as the most powerful politician in the country, he allowed himself to be kept by rich men. Truth, probity, self-reliance – these were all dull civic virtues he obviously felt should not be expected of a prince.

And yet, for all his notions of himself, you felt he was never confident of making it on his own merits. Take 1970, when there was astonishment that Haughey was mixed up in the events that led to the Arms Trial. Of the three ministers who left Jack Lynch's government on 6 May 1970, Blaney and Boland were convinced Republicans who were ready to pay the political cost, face the political wilderness – but Haughey knew he'd made a career mistake. John Healy caught Haughey's dilemma in his Backbencher column the following Saturday.

Referring to the departure of the three ministers as like a Soviet public trial, Healy said: 'But it was only in Ireland and in an Irish situation you could find one of the accused on the backbenches, smiling broadly. It didn't take a feather out of Neil Blaney .... Charles Haughey, who had limped in half-drugged to the secret trial in the party room, was driven home and did not appear for the farce of the formal indictment.' Healy went on: 'I never saw a happier pair of political corpses on Wednesday night than Neil Blaney, or Kevin Boland. Charlie was the only one of the trio with the Chappaquiddick look about him.'

(John Healy, *The Irish Times*, 9 May 1970, 'Backbencher')

Playing with republican fire as a way of political advancement was high risk. It blew up in his face. It dogged him, as had Chappaquiddick dogged Senator Ted Kennedy, for the rest of his political career. It was a risk he didn't have to take.

This man had great attributes – intelligence, insight, vision. He would have succeeded no matter what he tried to do. He never needed to make the compromises he made – not just the gifts of money he accepted but the raucous appeals to the republican fringe; the promotions given to underpowered backbenchers who supported his bid for leadership; the constant reliance on a sycophantic court; the cheap political strokes.

It would all have fallen into his lap anyway – not the racehorses and the island and the mansion, maybe, but he would almost certainly have become Fianna Fáil leader and Taoiseach. What's more, he would have taken office without dividing his party, but with the respect which allowed him to do much more than he did, much earlier.

The tragedy is not that he failed us. The real tragedy is that he failed himself.

BERTIE

Yer Man

There's a man sitting on the wall outside Hardwicke Street flats. Sometimes you see him in Dominic Street or Saint Mary's Place. He sits on the wall on Saturday afternoons, chatting to the passers-by, waving at the children. He's one of the local characters.

On Mondays he hangs around the schools. A principal arriving to open his school at 8.30 on Monday morning will find him waiting outside the gates. He'll chat to the principal and greet the parents as they leave their children to school. Sometimes they're nice to him. Sometimes they shout at him and put him down. He just smiles with his big sad eyes and shuffles on. After all, he's only a Taoiseach.

His Special Branch men stay well out of sight. Dublin Central isn't the sort of constituency where it pays to get above yourself. You have to knock on doors and take what comes. You have to be down on the street with everybody else. When *The Irish Times* ran a picture of our Bert in his wellies standing sadly in the middle of a flooded Richmond Road, his national handlers went ballistic – it wasn't dignified. But down at the East Wall, they loved it. Bertie was sharing in their misery.

Because he belongs to them. And they take it personally when the media sneer at him. Take the spelling story, where *The Irish Times* ran a photograph of Bertie's misspelt entry in the book of condolences for George Best. Out in the constituency they were proud that a guy who forgot to put the 'h' in sympathies had become Taoiseach, like they were proud that Curtis Fleming from Ballybough played for Middlesbrough and Ireland. Anyway, as Bertie told me years ago, there are only three copies of *The Irish Times* read in his constituency. 'We've worked out who buys the first two,' he said grimly, 'and we're still working on the third.'

He loves his constituency. Why wouldn't he? If you were writing a children's story about the ideal taoiseach's constituency, could you do any better? Look at the name: Dublin Central. Look what it includes: O'Connell Street, the Liffey, the Phoenix Park, the Zoo, the Botanic Gardens. People from Dublin Central regard themselves as the real Dubs, as East Enders think they're the real Londoners. They look down on Southsiders as fake and pretentious and that goes across all classes. A doctor's son from the Northside told me: 'We regarded the Southside as posh and full of Jesuit schools. We even dismissed Belvedere College as a sort of Southside colony.'

In Dublin Central you have to be local, down to earth, and preferably working-class. That's why locals think Sinn Féin may have overshot the mark by parachuting in

Rathgar-born, middle-class Mary Lou McDonald to replace Cabra's favourite son, bricklayer Nicky Kehoe. Nicky got an impressive 5,000 or so first preferences last time, and missed a seat by about only 80 votes because he didn't get transfers. His years in jail for the attempted Galen Weston abduction came against him, but the expected increase in Sinn Féin's vote would surely have put him in next time. Was it really necessary for the party to go for clean-skin McDonald?

She'll find this is one of the toughest constituencies in the country. Firstly, there's Bertie's legendary constituency machine: eight full-time workers, costing the taxpayers nearly a quarter of a million a year, and an army of ward bosses, each minding two or three streets in the constituency. There's a story that Christy Burke of Sinn Féin set out proudly to canvass in one election flanked by forty workers, many of them from Northern Ireland – only to meet Bertie coming around the corner with over a hundred. Ahern tends this constituency like a constant gardener and sets such a pace of openings and appearances on Mondays that his fellow TDs just spend all day on a roll following him.

Secondly, in Dublin Central, as we've said, they love a local. In the middle of a sharp political row in the Dáil recently with Labour's Róisín Shortall, Bertie suddenly interjected, 'and I have the greatest respect for Deputy Shortall.' When I asked Róisín afterwards to explain, she laughed and said: 'We grew up together. I'm from

Drumcondra. Out there, it doesn't go down well to attack your own.'

Thirdly, there'll be lots of competition. Tony Gregory, born in Ballybough, is now embedded. The Gregory Deal – the massive cash injection he negotiated for the poorer parts of this constituency as the price of supporting Charles Haughey's minority government in 1982 – as well as all his subsequent work have built him up a loyal following. Deputy Joe Costello of Labour, who lives in Aughrim Street, has done community work and prisoners' rights work in the area for decades. They, along with Bertie, and perhaps the Greens' Patricia McKenna who lives in the area, will be dipping into the same left vote as Sinn Féin's McDonald.

So have Sinn Féin made a mistake in not sticking with their local son? They may have or they may, on the other hand, have noticed something others haven't come to terms with. Dublin Central is gaining a whole new immigrant population. Many of them in time will have votes and they won't have the area's traditional loyalties.

But more important right now is the fact that this constituency is fast becoming apartment-land. From the Point Depot all down along the North Quays, and all around the Phoenix Park, there are new gated apartments. No one can go in to canvass. No one knows where the residents are from or if they vote at all. But, potentially, they could account for up to a quarter of the vote. In the local Brunswick Street School polling station in the last general election, there had been only four votes cast by five in the afternoon. 'Your only way in to these people is through radio and television, through 'Questions and Answers' or the 'Vincent Browne Show' said one local TD. 'They're locked away inside their apartment buildings.'

And maybe that's what the Shinners have spotted: a whole new television-bound electorate for media-friendly Mary Lou, all of them young, mobile and totally oblivious to the nice man with the sad eyes sitting on the wall outside.

Seeing Red

The organisers of an adult literacy conference in Dublin were understandably delighted that the Taoiseach had agreed to launch it. They wanted to make the most of their important guest and have him make a grand entrance. Their idea was that we'd all stand up. I, as conference chairperson, would announce the Taoiseach, who would then march in as we all clapped. So we all stood up. But before I could say a word, Bertie Ahern did a quick runner up the side of the room and slid into a chair beside me whispering, 'Howaya.' No pomp and ceremony. It's not Bertie's style.

And it's this matter of style which comes to the fore when you're talking about Bertie's declaration that he's a socialist. What he's really saying is: 'I'm an ordinary Joe.' And that's what resonates with most people who haven't time to read their Marx or their Gramsci. If he dresses like me and sounds like me, and enjoys the ordinary things I enjoy like football and pints, then he must be on my side. Yeah, but is he a socialist?

Well, he has, it's true, a Stalinist ability to airbrush from history those he's purged. Gone is Charlie McCreevy, waving his ideological sword at reds and lefties. Instead, pouring comfort into your ear on RTÉ's 'Morning Ireland' is modest Brian Cowen. 'We're not an uncaring crowd,' says Brian stoutly, promising he will give as generously as he possibly can to families, to the disabled and those who need medical cards. Add to that the iconic caring figure of Father Seán Healy starring at Fianna Fáil's Inchadoncy conference and welcoming every budget since; not to mention the public recanting by Séamus Brennan of his deviationist rightwing tendencies. Top it all with Comrade Bertie on every available TV channel and front page chanting the words 'socialist', 'republican', 'caring' and your repositioning is half done. And, of course, Pat Rabbitte protests about it and we all write about it, which gives it even more currency. And Labour looks on with a mixture of admiration and despair as the Taoiseach slides shamelessly left onto their ideological perch and says: 'Eh, howaya.'

But for all their outrage, Labour can learn lessons from Bertie and his new-minted version of municipal social- ism. First, be positive, always positive. Second, look at how he sells his idea of socialism, however insubstantial they judge it. Bertie paints a picture into which people can put themselves. 'It is a fact that the richest family in this area can on a Sunday afternoon go to the Botanic Gardens and the poorest family can too. And they can both share the same things. So I have fought for fifteen years to improve the resources of things like that: the

Phoenix Park, Dublin Zoo …' he's said. Gramsci couldn't have put it better: pleasure gardens for the people – happy, beautiful, fun places, places we all have access to, places with flowers and trees and children and animals. These are the places Bertie uses to symbolise his brand of municipal socialism. He's a master of the positive image.

And if 'socialist' means 'ordinary', he wears the label well. Charlie Haughey aside, ordinariness is house-style for Fianna Fáil. Fellas might like the opera or objets d'art, but they don't talk about it. They might all read *The Irish Times*, but publicly they sneer at it – Bertie in particular – as pretentious and upper-class. Socialist Noel Browne often told me that he felt much more at home with Fianna Fáil than Fine Gael for that reason. 'In their way, they represent the *gnáth-daoine*,' he said, 'the ordinary people.'

No one can deny Bertie's genuine interest in trade union issues. He was centrally involved in setting up and maintaining the social partnership process, and as Minister for Labour established the Labour Relations Commission. As Finance Minister he took quiet pleasure in reining in tax relief on company cars and meals out, and business people told me it was no surprise to them he was calling himself a socialist. 'Sure, he's handed over the running of the country to the Irish Congress of Trade Unions,' said one. 'He stopped the privatisation of the public sector,' said another, 'and then rewarded the public sector unions with benchmarking without demanding any reform. Yeah, he can call himself a socialist.'

So how does all this fit with being the Finance Minister who introduced the last tax amnesty? The Taoiseach who has created more Irish multimillionaires than any other in the history of the state? The man who presides over a country where many rich people pay no tax or little tax; where the taxes that hurt rich people most are low or non-existent (corporation tax, capital gains tax, property tax), while the taxes everyone, including the poor, has to pay are high (VAT, excise, local authority charges, car tax); where income tax rates may look low, but where people not too far above the average industrial wage are hitting the higher rate of 42%; where in inner city schools, like in his own constituency, many kids don't complete secondary level and almost none go to third level; where there are still dangerous queues in A and E; where tribunals into corruption are disclosing close links between developers and mainly Fianna Fáil figures; where rich business men like Des Richardson raise money for this truly socialist Taoiseach and where he mingles happily with the richest of Irish multimillionaires in the Fianna Fáil tent at the Galway Races?

And indeed how ordinary is a man who lives a life totally in the political arena; who never takes public transport and who has been cosseted by state-provided cars for so long that only recently he discovered his driving licence had expired without him noticing it?

There's no doubt that this is a prosperous society, one in which more Irish people than ever are materially better off. However, there are many tests of what might constitute a socialist or even a social democratic society and an obvious area is adequate provision of public services like health and education. That's where Bertie's socialist claims wear most thin. That's where the two tier nature of Bertie's Ireland is all too clear. Maybe he lives modestly. Maybe he sounds and looks like a man of the people. But is he really just an ordinary capitalist running dog ... in an anorak?

ENDA

Iron in the Soul

There was a moment in the Dáil when you realised that the iron had finally entered his soul. It was three years into his leadership and he was pushing the Taoiseach on the full cost of the disastrous PPARS computer system for the Department of Health. Bertie, trying to blind him with a mass of figures, sneered: 'I know the sums sometimes come as a problem to Deputy Kenny.' Kenny snapped back: 'At least I did not falsify my degree.'

We sat up. At last the mouse had roared. Not that they were fighting over much – Enda's national teacher qualification and first Arts in UCG as opposed to Bertie's curriculum vitae mentioning UCD and the London School of Economics, from which others might infer he had taken degrees. But it was an interesting clash because of what it revealed: firstly, that Fianna Fáil will set out to bully Kenny unmercifully in an election campaign because of his lack of experience in the economic area; secondly, that Kenny won't easily be bullied and that he's going to make a big point of the fact that he has nothing to hide. He had no links with the Haughey era. He had no appearance at the tribunals. A clean record then, but is it also a totally blank one?

Because this is the man who came from nowhere. He's personable, good with people, charming, but what did he do with his fifty-one years before he became leader of Fine Gael in 2002? Pulled out of his second year in UCG to contest a by-election when his very popular father, Deputy Henry Kenny, died, he had over ten years as an undistinguished backbencher; a year as a Minister for State in the eighties; and two years as Minister for Tourism and Trade in the nineties. Tourism and Trade did well in those years, but the development he will be remembered for are the tax reliefs for building houses in traditional holiday resorts including Westport and Achill in his own constituency, and Enniscrone on the edge of it. These were generally regarded by environmentalists as a disaster, a blot on the fragile landscape of places like Achill. Frank McDonald of *The Irish Times* has been scathing about the 'Toblerone Cottages' built in such scenic areas. In the end, well-off investors made a killing, but locals found that land prices were pushed up and that there was no long-term employment gain. There are other things for which he'll be remembered locally, like his role in bringing the Cable Products and APC plants to his home town of Castlebar, giving jobs to over 300 people.

But all of that does not amount to a glittering career. It was only Fine Gael's self-destruction in 2002 which allowed Enda to emerge as the last man standing. Of course there was Richard Bruton, who probably had the biggest single bloc of support but who, because of associations with his brother's regime, couldn't have united the party. In the end, Enda was the only one left who could lead or had the heart to lead. Fine Gael had chosen a man with no past, and, it looked at the time, no future. But Enda has surprised them all.

He's already done a superb job with the party. It's united. Membership is up, particularly among young people. Party funds are flush, business money is flowing in, and everything's in place for the election. His series of public meetings around the country worked well and he's warm and easy with people. His new resolution, he says, is to spend thirty seconds extra with everyone he meets.

Standing on the plinth outside the Dáil before the summer recess, he was waiting for Sky News to come through to him to do an interview live on air. As they started to count him in from the studio, a man passed by, recognised him and rushed over. 'Have you a second to say hello to my mother-in-law?' asked the man. 'Sure,' said Enda happily 'I have thirty seconds.' As the handlers fretted, he chatted to the woman and then turned straight to the cameras and did his piece. You always find time for a voter.

His Dáil performances have improved – the backroom boys have been working on him. When he started in 2002, he was abysmal. His party colleagues would shift uneasily in their seats, or become engrossed in their papers as Enda attempted to take on the Taoiseach. He couldn't seem to get it right. Either he was too tentative and oblique, or he indulged in wild hyperbole – and his embarrassed smile indicated that he knew why the government benches were jeering him. But the handlers took him aside. They worked to tidy up his naturally discursive turn of phrase, his indirect way of putting things, maybe a west of Ireland habit. They encouraged him to use short, clear sentences, to come straight to the point, to repeat the short direct message, the sound bite. Bertie may regret his decision to run the full five-year government term. That extra time has been invaluable in the shaping of Enda.

Now he's focussed. When he speaks, his own deputies look at him and listen. He no longer smiles apologetically at Bertie but looks him straight in the eye. And the Bert isn't so nice to him any more. Bertie curls up like a coiled spring, head down, eyes staring at his big black shoes, just as he does when Pat Rabbitte questions him. Indeed, recently, attacking Fine Gael's bill proposing that home owners should have more powers of self-defence against intruders, Bertie went as far as to accuse Kenny of being 'populist'. As political endorsements go, Kenny could hardly have hoped for better.

Mind you, this criminal-bashing stuff is not pretty politics. But it's what a lot of voters want. And in that, Kenny is following to the letter Flannery's Yellow Brick Road –

that's the report that long-time Fine Gael guru and ex-head of The Rehab Group, Frank Flannery, and others, drew up for Kenny in 2003.

The report of the Fine Gael Strategy Review Group is one of the sharpest, best written, and cynical works of political analysis ever to inform the Irish political debate. Some would label it as realistic, not cynical. Basically it says you give the people what they want: 'We are not telling them what they like or what they should like – they are telling us.' It says that the era of policy-driven politics is long gone, that politics are increasingly personality/people driven and that the leader is key. Instead of traditional appeals to idealism or class, the appeal is now to the senses, i.e. whether people feel good about the leader. 'In a word, politically, we have passed, to some degree, from substance to shadow – we are dealing not just with ideology, but also with image.' The report goes on: 'A lousy party can succeed with a brilliant leader – the opposite does not work.'

It warns that in a consumer age, politicians have to deliver simple, easily marketable messages, have to realise that people will select or discard them as mercilessly as they do any other product and it concludes: 'Where once politicians were philosophers, social engineers and idealists, now they are market strategists, brand-managers and salesmen.'

One shouldn't be surprised that a political party should be so wearily pragmatic – only surprised, perhaps, because it's stolid old upright Fine Gael. Anyway, Enda has stuck rigorously to the programme. As well as constant focus groups, he's asked the people at public meetings around the country what they want and they've told him. So he has three simple messages: he'll be tough on crime; he'll end the scandal of patients on trolleys; he'll stop the waste of taxpayers' money. That's it. He repeats those three points in every interview, every speech, every time he stands up in the Dáil. Those messages are emblazoned under giant posters of him all over the country. Enda – blonde, blue-eyed, fit and fresh – and three messages on crime, health and waste. That's the package so far. Simple.

Can it work? Can he win? Well, sometimes, you don't have to win. You just have to be there when a tired government loses. And there's a real tiredness about this government now, a been-around-too-long, same-old-faces syndrome, a feeling that, like the hapless Frank Spencer in 'Some Mothers do have 'em', they've had to say sorry once too often.

Critics may dismiss Kenny as just a likeable guy – or, as someone put it to me recently, a Robert Redford Lite, physically attractive, mentally anaemic. But the truth is that being liked is important in politics. And there's something even more important at which Enda has shown he's very good indeed – elections. Fine Gael's results in the European and local elections and their by-election win in Meath are witness to that.

Still, as his face flashes again across the television screen, with hardly a wrinkle or a heavy political thought to furrow his tanned, blonde brow, I'm reminded again of Robert Redford's character in 'The Candidate'. It's the ultimate film about the triumph of political style over substance. They gamble all to win, and win they do. And then, power in his hands at last, the victorious Redford turns around and asks helplessly: 'What do we do now?'

Beware the Erogenous Zone

Every party has its erogenous zone, the spot which, when stroked, delivers a passionate reaction. And you always know that a party conference speech has hit that spot when you get more than applause. You get the throaty roar.

With every party that sweet spot is different. With the PDs, it's tax. With Labour, it's equality. With Fianna Fáil, it's Irish unity. With Fine Gael, it's law and order. Watching the Fine Gael party leader's speech at the 2006 Ard-Fheis, there was a good reception for all his comments on health – but nothing like what greeted him when he said: 'When the law-and-order party is back in power, the thugs will be out of business.' God almighty, it was blood-curdling. And it was surpassed only by the roar when he proposed changing the law so people defending their homes against intruders wouldn't be sued. Law and order AND property. There's no headier mix for a Fine Gael crowd. They were ecstatic.

Because law and order and property, says everything about who Fine Gael are and were. They were traditionally the farming and the propertied classes favoured by a particular set of laws and a particular sort of order. And, as is the case with most erogenous zones, law and order brought out the best and the worst in them. They were the first government of the State. They set up the police and the army and defended the State, as they would see it, against republican subversives. Good. But after they were voted out of power in 1932, it may have been their law and order tendencies which led them to elect as leader of their newly merged party the proto-fascist and Blueshirt leader, Eoin O'Duffy. Bad.

Liam Cosgrave did the State some service on a law-and-order issue in 1970. As opposition leader, his letter to Jack Lynch forced into the open the events which led to Lynch's sacking of his ministers and to the Arms Trial. Good. But in power, Cosgrave's government presided over the repressive activities of the Garda so-called Heavy Gang. Bad.

Listening to the crowd baying at Enda's promises to lock up A and E drunks in drunk tanks, to tag electronically people he calls thugs, to force judges to explain themselves if they dared to give sentences other than those laid down by politicians, I thought: bad. Bad Enda. And for two reasons. Good Enda as an image has been working quite well. And that's Kenny as he is – a decent man, generous to colleagues and opponents, a reconciler.

I wrote a column about him recently, saying he was a lightweight like the Robert Redford character in the film 'The Candidate'. In the Dáil lobby later that week, an arm went round my shoulder. 'I liked the Robert Redford bit,' confided Enda. 'As for the rest, I'll have to go back and watch the end of the movie.' And then he headed cheerfully off down the corridor. No offence. Nice guy.

That's why the stuff he was peddling at the Ard-Fheis didn't sit easily on him. He's not a little Hitler and the whole performance didn't do any favours for him or Fine Gael. No party should want its annual conference to come across like the Tory Party in the Thatcher/Tebbit days.

But there's something else. For all its faults, Fine Gael has always been fairly realistic. That realism is one of the core differences between itself and Fianna Fáil. It's as though the two parties take their inspiration from two different sources. Fianna Fáil is loyal to the nation and a 32-county dream. Fine Gael is loyal to the State and a 26-county reality. Electorally, almost always, the dream won out.

Still, the people periodically would turn to Fine Gael for that very realism. Because generally, until the last election, when it made promises to everybody from taxi drivers to Eircom shareholders, the party took pride in not promising what it couldn't deliver on. But Enda Kenny's calls in his Ard-Fheis speech for drunk-tanks, tagging, effectively mandatory sentences, were ugly and empty threats. They were unrealistic. Constitutionally, almost none of them can be delivered on. They just sound tough.

There is a real law-and-order issue out there and at a time of flux and change, people need reassurance. The way to give them reassurance is through a reformed and expanded Garda force with a mission to serve the community and a solid presence in the community – whether that's in rural Ireland or in the heart of the cities. A policy aimed at knitting the gardaí back into the community would be a real service to law and order. Enda Kenny didn't have a word to say about it in his speech.

So yes, Enda. There are some Fine Gael traditions worth drawing on. Sober realism, being straight with the voters, is one. Whipping up a Fine Gael crowd to bay at a law-and-order moon, is not.

BRILLIANT CAREERS

Ex Ray

Don't put yourself up for auction. It can be a shock to discover how little you're worth. It happened to me once. Then Minister for the Environment, the late John Boland of Fine Gael, asked a bunch of us from RTÉ out to a 'do' in his North Dublin constituency, to be auctioned for charity.

Two actresses from the then new soap, 'Glenroe', did really well – the money came rolling in. Then it was my turn and, despite the best efforts of the auctioneer, there were no takers. I stood on the stage, my smile getting tighter and tighter, staring hopefully at the audience who stared disinterestedly back at me. Out there was a jungle of North Dublin politicians, with whom I'd had many a tangle in the comfortable security of the television studio. Now I was at their mercy, on their ground. I was feeling more and more like the *spailpín fánach* when suddenly a man at the back of the hall called out a bid, and every head turned to look at him respectfully. Then, as though he'd given them a cue, they all started to bid and soon I was sold for a respectable amount to the opening bidder, Deputy Raphael Burke. Yes, Raybo was my saviour.

It was a courtesy that I never totally forgot, despite the sharp exchanges we had over the years. Ray was a complex man, sometimes a saviour, always a bully. You were aware first of his physical bulk and that's how he wanted it. He swung into every situation shoulders first, chest forward like a fighter. A constituency colleague remembers how, at openings and public events locally, Ray would stand right in front of representatives from other parties when the photographs were being taken. Barrel-chested as he was, he could block them totally. Another remembered turning up to a local event that Ray, then a minister, had hoped to hog for Fianna Fáil. The opponent's hand was seized by Ray in a bone-crushing grip and Ray's fist pummelled his shoulder. 'You're very welcome to a Fianna Fáil function,' said Ray, but his fist pounded home the real message.

He made little attempt to hide his hostility to RTÉ when he was Minister for Communications. He backed enthusiastically the opening of a new commercial radio station and he capped RTÉ's advertising revenue. Once, he told my then 'Today Tonight' editor, Peter Feeney, that Feeney's career would go no further as long as he, Ray Burke, was Minister for Communications. If it was meant as a joke, it was a very pointed one.

He cornered me in the Dáil restaurant in the eighties, at a time when we journalists were reporting on moves in the party to dislodge Charles Haughey. I was doing a mixture of broadcasting for both RTÉ and BBC at the time. 'I hope you're declaring all of this for tax now,' he said meaningfully. 'I hope the taxman is fully aware of all your activities.' 'Well, since it all went out on air,' I snapped, 'I was hardly trying to hide it.' This is the man convicted of failing to declare over £100,000 for tax in the eighties and nineties. At the time, I thought he was impertinent. Now I know he was outrageous.

But then Ray always got his retaliation in first. He was part of a North Dublin mafia whose god was Charlie Haughey. If Ray voted against Haughey in the late seventies, that was because Ray, as a junior minister then, decided his future was best served by sticking with the establishment candidate, George Colley. Through the eighties, he and Bertie Ahern were regular guests up at Haughey's Kinsealy mansion. They thrived on machismo and on an us-against-the-world belief that North Dubliners, real Dubs, were your only men. Country-and-Westerners like Albert Reynolds were seen as inter-lopers. Sacked by Albert, Burke knew his pal Bertie would reinstate him and I never saw a happier man than Burke as he bounded up the stairs to the Dáil chamber the morning Albert made his resignation speech. 'The Praetorian Guard,' he purred to me, 'is changing.'

Bertie defended him passionately and for a long, long time. What is it about these North Dubs that they stick together so fiercely? Ray isn't saying.

In fact, so far Ray's said nothing. He hasn't involved colleagues and he hasn't involved family. Those down at the court when he was sentenced to six months in jail noticed that Ray stood alone. There was no public show of family members and that was brave of him – to decide to take the rap alone, to leave his family out of it.

And as he marched out of court in true Fianna-Fáil-at-Bodenstown fashion and climbed impassively into the prison van, I suppose there were few of us who didn't feel a twinge of sympathy for him and his family. The court was right and this was an important and historic decision which makes it clear that justice will indeed be done even to the powerful.

But if any of us were to make his mistakes and end up behind bars, maybe we'd want people to remember the small courtesies as well as the big crimes. Maybe we'd hope they might say: 'She was kind to me once,' or 'He was kind to me once.'

And he was.

So. Farewell Then

I was sitting beside John Bruton once listening to Paul
Durcan read his famous poem, 'The Hay Carrier', about
the Durcan family's origins in Mayo. From the stage, the
poet inimitably intoned the lines:

I am a hay-carrier
My father was a hay-carrier
My mother was a hay-carrier
My brothers were hay-carriers …

John Bruton was getting more and more perplexed
and suddenly he leaned across me to his wife and said:
'Hey, Finola, what's he talking about? Sure, wasn't his
father a judge on the Western Circuit?'

And that was our John. A plain man – not big on the
fancy stuff. He never lost the naïveté of a life lived only in
politics. But within that political world, which began for
him when he first entered the Dáil at the age of twenty-
two, he was a powerhouse of knowledge and ideas. He
read deeply on European social and economic policy. He
even spoke passable French. But the wider world, you
felt, was a bit of a mystery – like the world of literature.
He once announced to Edna O'Brien that he couldn't

give her an interview because she wasn't an accredited Dáil political correspondent. As to music ... well, at a Dublin concert celebrating John McCormack, he announced enthusiastically to friends: 'Now, this ... THIS is my kind of music.'

And in a way, John McCormack was the perfect accompaniment to Bruton's world: a world touched by sepia, in which a fella had two navy blue suits, one for Sunday; a world in which the main meal was in the middle of the day and had lots of red meat; a world in which Fine Gaelers lived on the farm or over the shop. It was also a world in which loyalty to family and land were paramount, and in which Irish Parliamentary Party leader, John Redmond, and his successors John Dillon and eventual Fine Gael leader, James Dillon, were the natural icons.

Bruton was a product of this world, and its willing prisoner. Redmond shaped his views on the North. The Christian Democrats shaped his view of social and economic policy. More than any other minister in the 1980s coalition with Labour, he fought Dick Spring to defend Fine Gael against Labour's socialist ideas. That bull-headedness and his refusal to go into government with the Stalinist Democratic Left lost him the chance to be Taoiseach in 1993.

When Bruton did get his chance in 1994, he had learned his lesson. He handled Labour with kid gloves, so grateful was he to be Taoiseach.

Still, the old Redmondite showed through. There was his heavy-handed wooing of unionists and his backing of Northern Secretary Sir Patrick Mayhew's insistence on prior IRA decommissioning at a sensitive time for the peace process. There was his embarrassing speech claiming that Prince Charles' visit to Ireland marked 'the happiest day of my life'. When the state of Victoria in Australia was celebrating its bi-centenary, the Irish cabinet wanted as a goodwill gesture to send it the old statue of Queen Victoria which used to stand outside Leinster House. But Bruton objected to giving away 'part of our heritage'. 'So you'll erect it in the main street of Navan, will you, before the next general election?' asked a Labour colleague. Bruton saw the point and let the statue go.

He was always conscious of himself as a Christian Democrat. When Ruairí Quinn suggested that a casino would help make a national conference centre self-financing, Bruton said his Christian Democratic values wouldn't allow it. When Quinn as Finance Minister proposed tax relief on childcare for working couples, Bruton said no. As a Christian Democrat Prime Minister, he would never discriminate against the woman in the home, he said.

It will stand to him that he held that coalition together well. It will stand to him that he was a man of ideas – the present Dáil Committee system, which gives a real edge to parliament, is his legacy. Sometimes, though, you wondered if he was more interested in drawing up policy papers, than getting into power to implement them. He seemed more comfortable in opposition than any proper politician should be, busy producing a library full of policy documents instead of straining every nerve to fight, crawl, wheedle his way back into power.

Still, his policy drafting skills stood to him when he was on the convention which helped to draw up Europe's Constitution. And that, as well as his high standing with the powerful European Christian Democrats group, guaranteed him his new job as the EU's man in Washington. How will he get on there? He should be fine. It's a pols' city and he's a pol.

And he has his place in history – he's been Taoiseach, something many of us did not expect, nor did he. 'He was like a helium balloon for two whole years,' said bemused Labour ministers. 'We had to pull him down from the ceiling.' Indeed, on the night he was elected, he drove home to his beloved Cornelstown in County Meath, and a reporter with a camera asked him how it felt to be Taoiseach. He just broke into the famous laugh, a laugh of pure raucous delight, a child's laugh as Paul Durcan beautifully described it. He had a child's taste in food, too, and had no problem hopping out of the ministerial car to get chips for himself and his driver. In Finance, he dined regularly round the corner in Burgerland.

In his final contribution to the Dáil, he made no self-serving speeches about himself, with quotes from

Shakespeare. Instead he made a daft joke about horizontal jogging, and then the great laugh brayed around the chamber for one last time. And maybe that was the happiest exit, not just for Bruton, but for a whole tradition which departed with him.

Or as EJ Thribb in *Private Eye* might have put it:

'*So. Farewell then*
John Redmond
James Dillon
John Bruton.'

Grumpy Young Men

Every so often in Dáil Éireann, the curtain parts and you get a glimpse of how things used to be, and how they may be again. It happened one Thursday when Brian Cowen took the Order of Business and suddenly you realised how accustomed we've got to the gentle life: to Bertie with his spaniel eyes, self-deprecating shrug, his please-like-me smile. Bertie makes a play of being helpful, even if the answers can be a bit hard to pin down. Bertie's the man who has put the word 'consensus' at the heart of politics. Even when it comes to the Opposition, Bertie loves to be loved.

Not so Brian Cowen. In twenty minutes that Thursday morning, you remembered how it was before: truculent, combative, take-it-or-leave-it 'cos we're the government. Great stuff for the Fianna Fáil troops. But how about the wider public watching? They're the ones Cowen will have to appeal to if he becomes leader of Fianna Fáil. And all they saw was an arrogant young man who chose to behave like a curmudgeonly relic of the past.

Cowen would put it differently. 'I'm a traditionalist,' he says. And to work out what that implies, it's worth

looking at his background and at a solid Fianna Fáil constituency where the party has held three of the five seats
for as long as anyone can remember. As a woman down
in Laois-Offaly said to me: 'Everything that needs to be
said about Brian Cowen is encapsulated in a word we
have down here and the word,' she said, laughing, 'is
"loylaty".' Well, 'loylaty' is a big word with us down in
Carlow as well: being loyal to your family, your place,
your party, and Cowen scores on all three. He dismisses
all jokes about Offaly. 'You simply don't understand us,'
he says loftily. 'We have reached a level of sophistication
that others can only aspire to.' He socialises down at
home, is an enthusiastic GAA supporter, both in Clara
where he was born and in the wider county. As Minister
for Foreign Affairs, he rushed home from the United
Nations to be at the launch of the Fleadh on a rainy day
in Tubber. Indeed, in Tubber, they would expect no less,
and that's why they love Brian Cowen.

He's a loyal son of the party and won the by-election at
the age of twenty-four after his father, Dáil deputy and
former junior Minister for Agriculture Bernard Cowen, died
suddenly. Ber was a close friend of Albert Reynolds and
had spent the snowy night before he died at Reynolds'
apartment in Dublin, where the two stayed chatting till four
in the morning. Brian was loyal to Albert, backing him in
his move against Haughey, and it was Albert Reynolds who
promoted him to the cabinet in 1992 and introduced him to
well-wishers as a future leader of Fianna Fáil.

When Albert was forced to resign, Brian Cowen was angry and showed it in an emotional performance on television. His subsequent bitterness against Dick Spring came through vividly at the Fianna Fáil Ard-Fheis of 1997 where he dismissed him as 'Clever Dick', 'Tricky Dick', 'Calamity Dick'.

And that's where they love him, at the heart of the party. He gets the sort of conference welcome from party members that once sealed Mo Mowlam's fate in the British Labour Party. He gets the same response in the parliamentary party and there's little doubt, given a vacancy, that they'd elect him leader in the morning. It's not just because he's great company, a brilliant mimic and a great man for a sing-song. They like his plain speaking, like when he told a journalist who asked if it was true he wanted to move out of Health: 'That's crap.' Or his muttered comment during long, drawn-out speeches at the negotiation of the Nice Treaty in December 2000: 'Wouldja ever hurry up. It's nearly Christmas!'

But most of all they love it when he lambastes the Opposition, like the old Civil War stuff he threw some years ago at Michael McDowell, who was attacking Fianna Fáil on the Opposition benches. 'What do you know about Fianna Fáil?' roared Cowen. 'Your whole seed, breed, and generation were anti-Fianna Fáil.' They loved it even more when he attacked his then reluctant PD coalition partners at the Fianna Fáil Ard-Fheis in 1992: 'If in doubt, leave them out.'

And the Fianna Fáil benches smiled on Thursday morning when he gave the Opposition one-line answers on the Order of Business, where deputies ask about forthcoming legislation. Bertie Ahern is expansive, gives explanations, ventures the odd opinion. Cowen just truculently read out the bare information deputies had already been sent by fax from the Whip's Office. 'It was monosyllabic, an exercise in minimalism,' said one. 'He was disdainful as he always is in dealing with the Opposition, as though the government knows best and shouldn't be disturbed.'

This is a bright man, an ambitious man, and a decent man, about whom, personally, even political opponents haven't a bad word to say. But he hasn't yet learned that leaders can't behave like corner-boys, particularly in a political age when they may be one day looking for coalition partners among the same Opposition parties they've dealt with so dismissively. Cowen's Dáil performance belongs to the bygone days of one-party government. That's why his Dáil performance came across as curiously old-fashioned and narrow, two words that should send a shiver down the spine of a catch-all party like Fianna Fáil.

If Fianna Fáil really intends that Brian Cowen should become Taoiseach of this country some day, maybe someone who loves him should take him aside and administer a few well-aimed kicks to his loyal Fianna Fáil posterior.

Grumpy Old Men

Do people vote for Grumpy Old Men? Maybe they do and maybe Pat Rabbitte's grumpiness is a calculated part of Labour's election strategy. But I have my doubts.

Being human, politicians will often be tetchy and irritated – but the golden rule is that they shouldn't show it in front of the cameras. It looks defensive. It looks as though you're not in control. Remember Michael McDowell and the Angry Pills. Clearly when you're defensive, you're not winning.

Nobody could be tetchier than Charlie Haughey. I remember him losing it on an election tour when the *Irish Independent* ran a headline suggesting he was chickening out on a TV debate with Garret FitzGerald. He called us all in to an as yet unopened and stale-smelling pub in Nenagh. He flung down the offending newspaper in front of me and asked me to explain myself. 'Not my paper, Mr Haughey,' said I. He snatched it up and flung it down in front of my friend from the *Indo*, who said: 'Not my story, Mr Haughey,' since the piece had been written in Dublin. Frustrated, Haughey stormed out of the pub and we fell around laughing and set to writing next day's piece about Mr Haughey being ever so cross. Yeah, we're a rotten lot.

But *we* don't matter! And Haughey knew that, which is why he never made the mistake of losing it in front of the cameras. He understood what so many politicians forget. The interviewer is merely the medium through which you talk to the voter. Never let the interviewer goad you into showing a side of yourself that you wouldn't want the voter to see. You're talking to Mrs Ryan or Mr Dunne in their sitting room or kitchen at home. Keep them in your mind all the time you're doing an interview. Would you be grumpy and irritable and tetchy if you were talking to them?

Rabbitte is good with voters and good on the stomp. He's warm and he listens and people like him. He's great in parliament. He's prepared, forensic, witty, and Bertie's head drops even lower and Bertie's duck's ass mouth tightens even further when Rabbitte gets up to speak. But put him in a television or radio studio and he gets tetchy. Of course interviewers should get their knuckles rapped now and then, but you sound defensive if you do it in a way which is bad-tempered. Rabbitte does this regularly. I've heard him do it on RTÉ's 'This Week' radio programme and again with Seán O'Rourke on RTÉ television's 'The Week in Politics'.

O'Rourke started off with a question about the empty seats in the Helix during Rabbitte's conference speech. He had put much the same question to Enda Kenny

about the empty seats at the Mill Street Fine Gael conference. The difference was that Enda shrugged it off. Pat
got cross. 'I think that is a pretty begrudging remark, if I
may say so,' snapped Pat. O'Rourke said it was what he
saw with his own eyes. 'I think it's a pretty begrudging
remark,' repeated Pat, who went on to point out that it
had been a most upbeat conference. And indeed it had.
So why did he start out by losing the cool about it?

Labour had cleverly used their television time not to
have potentially divisive debates on policy but to showcase their election candidates. Rabbitte's own speech had
an interesting piece of Tony-Blair-type distancing from
the unions. Yes, we would have liked more detail on
health policy and on Labour's solution to the scandalous
price of building land and of housing. But those policies
are promised.

So there was no reason to be on the back foot and yet
Rabbitte finished the interview by having another go.
Claiming that Labour and Fine Gael together would win
enough seats to go into government, he snapped: 'I
would point to the record of the commentators who,
right from Jack Lynch's result in 1977 until the results in
2002, got it gloriously wrong. And a little dollop of humil-
ity wouldn't do any harm for the commentators as they
purport to know what the outcome of an election will be
that probably won't be held until 2007.' Oh dear, who's
touchy, then? Who's feeling the pressure? Of course we
commentators goof. I remember writing a piece in 1994

about John Bruton's chances of government, headlined: 'He's down the end of Lonely Street, it's Heartbreak Hotel.' That was Sunday. Four days later he was elected Taoiseach.

So yes, we do get it gloriously wrong but *we* don't matter – or at least we matter only in as far as we are a link to the public. That link will be vital in this election year. A clever politician won't be diverted from his proper target by directing hissy fits at the interviewer, or at the media.

So don't get grumpy with us, Pat. It's true what they say, you know. There are no stupid questions – only stupid answers.

Losing it

Michael McDowell, they say, was a bright child, with a vivid imagination. He still is. Only someone with a very vivid imagination indeed could see the gentle Richard Bruton as Hitler's propaganda chief – Richard Bruton who is fair and courteous; who wears a smile of acute embarrassment at budget-time when he has to hurl at the government insults prepared for him by the Fine Gael speechwriters; who has long been criticised as being too nice for politics. When I put to it Bruton that he was the mildest of men, he groaned: 'I know, I know, I carry it around with me like a wooden leg.'

So Richard was woefully miscast. Michael McDowell himself was once referred to in a newspaper profile as being in appearance disturbingly like the Gestapo officer in the film 'Indiana Jones and the Raiders of the Lost Ark'. I'm sure he thought that was unfair. There are always dangers when you start opening the Nazi dressing-up box.

The irony is that this show of intemperance – all because Bruton said only two extra Guards were on Dublin's streets in 2005 – was indulged in by someone who represents the department of Justice, Equality and Law Reform; that he delivered it as he was arriving to open an event celebrating tolerance – Intercultural Week 2006. All he achieved was to give airtime to Fine Gael that they could only have dreamed of and which Richard Bruton used with precision and grace.

In other words, a mess. And this is where McDowell's barrister training lets him down. The skills honed in the L and H and in the Four Courts are all about talk, the louder and the more adversarial the better. The bigger the row, the better Michael likes it, and his Rottweiler's instinct is to attack. But sometimes in the Department of Justice, you're better to keep quiet. As the late Brian Lenihan said once, just do it. Don't stand around splashing in a puddle of self-righteousness. An excess of zeal is not always seemly in a Minister for Justice, Gerry Collins said when he held the office. It was Gerry who softened the profile of Portlaoise Prison, where the paramilitaries were held, by planting rose bushes all around it. Gerry argued the public didn't want to hear you talking about crime and prisons all the time. As long as you were doing your job, they just wanted you to get on with it.

The problem for McDowell is that he's been doing a lot of talking and yet people's fears about crime are top of the political agenda, as the opposition's focus groups keep telling them. The rash of gangland killings in Dublin, the panic over the striking out of the statutory rape law and the possible release of child-rapists, created a mood of national nervousness. People in that mood aren't reassured when the Justice Minister indulges in temper tantrums. The law-and-order minister should, above all, be calm.

Some restraint is exercised, even in our adversarial system of politics. Few enough politicians would have said, as Michael McDowell said in the Dáil to John Gormley of the Greens, that the gardaí had footage of the Progressive Democrats' Party offices being ransacked by a group of 'Deputy Gormley's type of people' during the 2006 Dublin riots. By this he meant muesli-eating sandal wearers. He withdrew that remark without much grace. The apology to Bruton, too, was fairly self-serving. 'I'm big enough,' he said, 'to admit that I have made a mistake.'

It's precisely this arrogance which gets up the nose of Fianna Fáil deputies. Said one: 'It's the way he looks up to heaven as though to say, God help me, I have to put up with ye.' He's not a team player, said another, and he announces things before he tells colleagues. Every so often he feels the need publicly to dismiss Fianna Fáil and Bertie reins him in by getting someone else at cabinet to deliver a curved ball. But generally they have a good relationship, bad cop, good cop. Michael takes a hard line on Sinn Féin and on immigrant control, something Bertie and Fianna Fáil are glad to hear said, but don't want to say themselves.

They've also come to accept his deeply-felt

nationalism. His grandfather was Eoin MacNeill and whatever Fianna Fáil might feel about MacNeill's countermanding of the Easter Rising, he was President of the Irish Volunteers. MacNeill's son, Michael's uncle Brian, was shot dead on the Republican side in the Civil War in Sligo and Michael keeps in his office the flag draped on his uncle's coffin.

He makes it clear he's impatient to be leader of his party but so far his ambitions have been stifled by Thelma and Louise. That's what he's reported to have called Mary Harney and Liz O'Donnell after losing his seat and leaving the party in a sulk in 1997. He reportedly said he'd never work with them again. But back he came only to find that they are now no easier to push around than they were before.

And there's a reason why. Michael may be a brilliant senior counsel, but the women are seasoned politicians. Neither of them has ever lost her seat – rule number one in politics. And when it comes to understanding leadership battles, well, Mary Harney could write the handbook on that one. She learned all about it in close combat with Charlie Haughey.

But O'Donnell particularly gets under his skin and does it all the time, part of an old hostility which goes back to the time that McDowell first lost his seat (he does make a habit of it) in Dublin South East in 1989. Michael, subsequently, did not deign to run for a mere council seat in the area but Liz did and won it, becoming the only

PD councillor on Dublin City Council. She was perfectly set up to run for the Dáil in South East but Michael insisted on being the candidate and Liz had to decamp, eventually finding a seat in Dublin South.

Unlike many politicians inside and outside the party, O'Donnell isn't afraid of McDowell and doesn't flinch at taking him on in argument. She's a lawyer herself; she knows the territory, and she takes a more liberal position on most issues than he does. She's put her foot down about a number of things. He wanted to lower the age of criminal consent to ten but met resistance within his own party when Liz insisted it remain at twelve. When he was advising the cabinet as attorney general up to 2002, the issue of having a citizenship referendum to close off the immigration loophole of babies born in Ireland was first raised. It went no further partly because Liz objected in principle.

But her sharpest shot across his bows came in 2004 when McDowell was at the height of his campaign against the continuing paramilitary and criminal activities of the Provisional Republican movement. Liz, former junior minister at Foreign Affairs and a veteran of the difficult negotiations for the Good Friday Agreement, warned that bashing Sinn Féin was not a good thing. A respectful approach to Sinn Féin had been more productive and had achieved more progress, she said sweetly.

O'Donnell's guerrilla war on McDowell may well reflect her own long-term leadership ambitions, but she also represents a genuinely more liberal view reflected by people like Deputy Fiona O'Malley, and by possible stars of the future like candidate Colm O'Gorman. Who knows what the party will look like after a general election and whether it will favour McDowell?

After all, he will be judged on his ministerial record. And while he has introduced a flurry of legislation, and has done well in the confrontation with prison-officers, his main job is to keep the streets safe for the citizen. In a country where homicides have risen by 300% in the capital in the last five years and where crime detection nationally over the same period has fallen, people don't feel so safe. That's why Richard Bruton drew blood on the Garda figures. Until recently at least, we were still short of the two thousand extra gardaí which were promised in 2002 and that's at a time when the population is increasing.

Sensitive on this point and wounded, McDowell struck out at Bruton and in the process, made a fool of himself, damaging his party and ministerial prospects. Once you become a political caricature, it's hard to be taken seriously again. And as McDowell fulminated to the gathered press outside Buswell's, angrily waving his bits of paper, and failing to answer the simple questions put to him, the journalists at the back began to snigger. 'It was so embarrassing,' said one, 'because we were watching someone lose it.'

And I wonder if he has even yet realised just how much he lost.

After the Revolution

The sad picture on the front of *The Irish Times* magazine told it all. Like wistful émigrés after the revolution, Charlie McCreevy and his wife Noeleen wandered through the frozen wastes of a Brussels park. Even before they'd fled the old country, the lefties had stormed the Winter Palace. There was nothing to go home to.

At home meanwhile, the party was imposing a new order. Gone were McCreevy's public celebration of wealth and enterprise, his attacks on pinkos like Fr Seán Healy. Now the Taoiseach had declared himself a socialist and Healy, or the anti-individualism guru, Robert Puttnam, attacked the old order at Fianna Fáil's September gatherings. Old capitalists publicly recanted, most prominent of all the once red-in-tooth-and-claw Transport Minister Séamus Brennan who, after an initial sulk, fervently embraced the department of Social Welfare and started chanting the mantra of the new regime: power to the people. In a notable Dáil speech peppered with phrases like 'responding sympathetically', 'reaching out', 'a rising tide which lifts those left behind', he concluded: 'My department is above all else about people. It must be people-centred.'

Only an apparition like Healy at Inchadoney could have brought about this level of conversion. This was Brennan, the macho market man who ate unions and heads of semi-state boards for breakfast. This was the man who said bullishly, 'Governments are there to do the job. Not to organise consensus.'

Yeah, well. Try sitting in on Dáil debates on social welfare these days.. There's lots of consensus being organised by Mr Brennan. Like when the Social Welfare Bill was in the Senate and he complimented all the Senators on their contributions and promised to discuss with them further. Like in the Dáil when he has opened his mind to opposition spokespeople and confessed to them that he was thinking of dropping current restrictions on lone parents. 'I have queried the advisability of having state officials enforcing a non-cohabiting rule when sensibly we should be encouraging both parents to look after the child. But instead state officials are forced by state policy to see that the father isn't in the house. And this in the twenty-first century! It's wrong for children. I don't like it. I'd welcome your thoughts on it.' Opposition spokespeople David Stanton of Fine Gael and Dan Boyle of the Greens and Willie Penrose of Labour looked a bit queasy at this close embrace, particularly Penrose, who prefers enough distance to be able to land a good left hook.

But the opposition Brennan and the government is

really concerned about for the moment is the constituency represented by Fr Seán Healy, and so far they've
delivered to him central demands: the increase in the
lowest rates of single social welfare payment in line with
the target set by the National Poverty Anti-Strategy to be
reached by 2007; the big increases on disability to be
delivered over the next few years; the reversal of many of
the so-called savage sixteen cutbacks introduced by Mary
Coughlan at Charlie McCreevy's insistence in 2002.
Brennan has also agreed with Healy about the need to
tackle child poverty and will be the Santa Claus responsible for handing out the extra 1000 euros annual payment
for young children from August 2006. And there have
been other issues like childcare places, and the setting up
of a new fund to support community organisations
which lost out in the reduction of community employment places, and the end of restrictions on the free travel
pass. The new trend is to be sensitive wherever there is
an issue of social inclusion, and he's been making sure
that language doesn't exclude people either. His 2006
Social Welfare Bill gets rids of the pejorative term 'old
age pensions', which will be now be called simply state
pensions. He's changed 'unemployment' benefit to
'jobseekers' benefit'.

It's the Zeitgeist. The nineties was McCreevy and the
market and shouting at Fr Seán Healy. The noughties is
caring and CORI and the Taoiseach spending more time
opening community centres in inner-city Dublin than in

the Fianna Fáil tent at Leopardstown.

And this conversion has nothing to do with God and everything to do with the electorate. The voters have already given Fianna Fáil a kick in the pants in the European and local elections – and anyway, as Séamus Brennan himself might say, it's a matter of numbers. Look how they stack up on the issue of whether a government should be pro-business or pro-welfare. There are 250,000 enterprises in the country, half of them one-person businesses. There are 970,000 social welfare recipients and one and a half million beneficiaries. You don't have to have a degree in political arithmetic to know which represents more votes.

Fianna Fáil's conversion was too late for the Meath and Kildare by-elections. The ravages of uncaring and unplanned economic growth cost them dearly there. But they're hoping that generous social welfare provision allied to the health of the economy will see them well-positioned for a general election. Central to that grand election plan will be the department Séamus Brennan turned his nose up at initially back in September 2004, a department which accounts for two-thirds of all government spending. And Brennan has embraced it with true zeal. No slouch when it comes to propaganda, he's even had Big Brother ads on the radio, reminding us where the largesse comes from. Haven't you heard them? Here's how one goes and I quote: 'The Department of Social and Family Affairs is committed to a caring twenty-first century social welfare service. Each week we are providing welfare benefits and vital support schemes that directly help well over one million people ...' And it ends: 'The Department of Social and Family Affairs – there when you need us.'

Ah!

Charlie McCreevy: eat your heart out.

There's Something about Mary

When Fianna Fáil won the 1977 election, their mighty landslide caused problems in all constituencies including that of the Taoiseach, Dún Laoghaire-Rathdown. Liam Cosgrave himself scraped in but it didn't look good for his long-standing FG colleague, the gentlemanly Church-of-Ireland deputy, Percy Dockrell. When Percy, in his leisurely fashion, arrived at the count, he was warned at the door he was in trouble. 'Oh no,' said Percy. 'Did Liam not get enough votes?'

That 1977 election changed a lot of things, including the tradition of a Protestant deputy for Dún Laoghaire, whether it was Fine Gael's Percy Dockrell or Fianna Fáil's Lionel Booth. For years not all that much had happened to disturb the even tenor of this area with its high percentage of non-Roman Catholic voters. Even still, according to the CSO, that vote is about 10%, well above the national average. This was the Royal Borough with its constant link to England through the mailboat. A British Queen and King visited, and many of the older post boxes, though now painted green, still carry a crown. This was a favourite retirement area for many ex-British army and navy people.

Twin steeples dominate the town – the Mariners' Church had to be built higher when a Royal visitor noticed that it was the Catholic steeple which dominated. These twin steeples told the story of a constituency which boasted a rich presence of both churches. The estates owned by Catholic religious institutions in the area must still account for a big percentage of Catholic Church wealth.

Much has changed from the time when Fine Gael's Percy Dockrell and Liam Cosgrave held the line here against dangerous leftie liberals – Cosgrave was so suspicious of lefties that even when talking to his Labour constituency colleague and coalition government partner, Barry Desmond, he could only refer to the Labour Party as 'your lot'. But now, from having once had three Fine Gael deputies, the constituency has none at all. It has voted consistently liberal on issues from divorce to abortion and had the highest 'no' vote in the country in the referendum to change the citizenship laws. Much of that independence of spirit is owed to Protestant dissenter tradition. And as for those liberals Cosgrave was so suspicious of, it has plenty of them now representing the constituency: Eamon Gilmore of Labour, Ciarán Cuffe of the Greens, Fiona O'Malley of the PDs and Barry Andrews of Fianna Fáil, two independent-minded backbenchers who have more than once questioned government decisions.

It's the perfect showcase constituency for Mary Hanafin, Fianna Fáil's face of the future. When it comes to ticking all the right Irish political boxes, Mary is a public relations dream. She's city (professional urban woman, former secondary schoolteacher in Sion Hill), but she's country (born in Tipperary). In this most liberal of liberal constituencies, she steers away from discussion on social issues like abortion. Yet everyone knows that her father is former Senator Des Hanafin, the anti-abortion campaigner, and she effortlessly hoovers up the two thousand or so local pro-life type votes.

Media handlers and producers love her. She's succinct. She knows her brief and, unlike her colleague Dick Roche, knows when to get off the stage. She's embedded in the party – her father was Fianna Fáil treasurer and she was joint treasurer. She was one of the most popular figures at the recent Ard-Fheis.

And when it came to a clash between the interests of the party and the leader, the Hanafins have been loyal to the party. Her father stood up to Charles Haughey – insisting on an audit before he handed over the party funds. She stood up to Haughey too. As a youngster on the national executive in 1985, in a public vote, Mary Hanafin refused to vote for Des O'Malley's expulsion from the party. She was one of the very few to do so.

She served her time as chief whip and gained widespread respect when despite the sudden death of her husband, barrister Eamon Leahy, she continued stoically to do her job, sitting white-faced behind the Taoiseach in the Dáil. Now she's Minister for Education, which is a good news department if you have money and don't annoy the teachers. So far she hasn't put a foot wrong. She balanced a public view that she was too much in the pockets of the teachers' unions by warning that teachers would lose pay if they left classes to attend the protest march against outsourcing in Irish Ferries in 2005. Mind you, this sounded braver than it was, since the money is unlikely ever to be collected.

But we really don't know her mettle yet because she hasn't been tested. It would have been interesting to hear her views on ending Church control of primary schools – the issue raised by the PDs' Liz O'Donnell after the report on sexual abuse of children by priests in the Diocese of Ferns. However, Bertie Ahern intervened quickly to stifle that debate so she hasn't had to step up to the plate in that or other contentious issues.

What we do know about is her vote-pulling ability. She works the constituency hard. She'll continue the balancing act, the mixed messages, which allow her to pull in the liberal and conservative, the secular and religious vote at once.

And she does it so well. On Ash Wednesday, as Ministerial colleagues flaunt their marks of penitence, Mary's brow is clear. One is discreet about such things in Dún Laoghaire. But when it matters, like when she's canvassing votes outside Glasthule Church, who is she flanked by? She's flanked by her father, former chairman of the pro-life amendment campaign. Has this woman the ability to be leader of Fianna Fáil? Oh yes, she has.

Little Willie

A constituent opened the door recently to Willie O'Dea. 'Lord, we thought you were dead, Willie,' he said. 'You haven't called to the house for a whole eight weeks.'

And that's Willie, the eternal canvasser, the man who offers perpetual succour to his Limerick constituents, always on the doorstep, always on the street, always on the job. And you can't miss Willie, a Charlie Chaplin figure with his moustache and his rolled-up umbrella, his trousers falling in folds over his big black shoes, and until recently anyway, a faint air of disappointment.

Then there's the walk, fast, head down. He walks everywhere in his constituency – you get seen that way. Last week, a local saw him walking along the Dock Road, against the backed-up traffic. 'I saw him. Everyone saw him. And that's the whole idea. He wanted to make it clear that nothing would change now that he's a minister. That's Willie.' Living as he does in a modest house off Henry Street in the heart of the city, nobody's ever seen Willie drive a car. He patrols his territory on foot and he guards each vote as a dog guards a bone.

He canvasses all the time, obsessively. It's said that the

Saturday after the 1997 election count, Willie was out again, knocking on doors. He only swapped his Saturday canvass for the rugby matches when he realised that that's where the votes were. He pulls in a big vote in the poorer areas of the city. No complaint is too small for him – windows, doors, pathways. At night he's in pubs like the Windmill, or South's or Tom Collins. He might only spend twenty minutes in each. He might have only two pints and ten glasses of water all night, but he's there.

Constituency colleagues over the years haven't enjoyed his methods, his way of working his own supporters into *cumainn*. For former Fianna Fáil colleague, Peadar Clohessy, one of the advantages of moving on to the PD ticket was that he got away from Willie. Willie sits like a clucking hen on his first preference vote which is always three times what his fellow Fianna Fáil TD Peter Power gets. Indeed in 1992, the imbalance was such that Fianna Fáil took only one seat, Willie's, and the PDs with a much smaller vote took two.

That behaviour doesn't go down well with Our Bert and probably accounts for the fact that Willie stayed a junior minister for thirteen whole years. He voted against Haughey in the gang of 22, but Haughey didn't rate him anyway and left him on the backbenches for twelve years. Hard for a bright man with accountancy and legal training, who lectured in Trinity and UCD in tax, commercial, company and property law and who is still on extended leave from the University of Limerick.

But the constituency is his strength and his weakness. He'll always be a constituency man first and a party man second. He marched against the closure of Barrington's Hospital and lost the party whip. And he could be what Jim Kemmy famously called 'mighty mouse in Limerick and dormouse in the Dáil.' When Limerick taximen were up in arms against Bobby Molloy's deregulation, he told the taximen in Limerick that he backed them, but voted for the measure in Dublin. Unfortunately for Willie, his inconsistencies at the Limerick meeting were caught on tape by RTÉ's Philip Boucher-Hayes. When he came into the Dáil to apologise, however, he did what he always did – he attacked first. Flailing at Fine Gael, he wondered if they would ever elect a leader more popular than the whooping cough and said that when John Bruton survived a putsch and was re-elected leader, it 'caused uninhibited celebration and joy in the households of every Fianna Fáil supporter from one end of Ireland to the other.'

His instinct is always to attack and he's good at raising the headlines, sometimes too good, like when he played the Wild Bill Hickok card, pointing a gun at the camera. The problem is he may be too colourful, too intemperate. A little more gravitas may be required if he's to move up from Defence.

Still, he's delighted at his promotion and so is Limerick. They were afraid he might throw himself off Sarsfield Bridge if he didn't get in this time, and even at the Galway races, Bertie was being berated by loyal Limerick matrons about it.

And Limerick likes his no-nonsense style. Many Ministers for Defence have worn hats and a previous holder of the office was spotted in Leonard's Men's Shop in Limerick practising holding his new hat over his heart, as one does when taking the salute. Not Willie who skipped through the rituals at Sarsfield Barracks with a bare head and not too much pomp.

Defence won't burden him. And for the rest of us, I suppose we can take some comfort in the fact that we'll always know where to find the man in charge of protecting the nation. He'll be protecting his constituency, marching down Limerick's Dock Road, armed to the teeth to repel all boarders with his moustache, his notebook, and his telescopic brolly.

When Garret was Eighty

Once, going to interview then Taoiseach Garret FitzGerald for *The Irish Times*, I had no one to mind the baby. 'That's all right,' said Garret when I rang him. 'Bring her with you.' It wasn't such a great idea. Half way through, with Garret dancing away from an awkward question, there was a little cry from the carrycot under the big mahogany table. Garret leaped to his feet and carolled: 'Baby awake. Interview over. Let's play with the baby.' And that's what he did, down on his hands and knees on the red dining-room carpet.

That was Garret: partly the big child; partly the cool political operator who'd take a convenient opportunity to avoid a difficult question.

We all knew the big child. Garret loved being with children, loved organising games and picnics for them. He kept his old children's story books, including girls' stories by writers like Rumer Godden. He loved ice-cream, and during election campaigns or even during breaks in the Dáil he could be seen sitting on a bench licking happily at his cone. When we travelled with him on election campaigns, he treated us as part of his extended family, standing on the steps of the departing bus and waving us on like a clucking hen. Mrs FitzGerald mothered us too, and she had a soft spot for the most wayward ones, particularly the suffering boys who'd stayed too long in the bar the night before.

They glowed in one another's company and they were together as much as they could be when he was Taoiseach and she was ill. Once at a British-Irish Association meeting in Oxford, they were given a twin-bedded room. Garret and Joan were having none of it. With the help of some Foreign Affairs aides, they reorganised all the furniture and pushed the two beds together.

Then there was the other side of Garret – the cool side. He thought emotion had no place in politics and was deeply mistrustful of the throaty roar of the crowd. He could be ruthless – he knew what had to be done to win power. He had read widely in the area of moral theology and had spent his gap year studying Thomist philosophy with the Jesuits in Belvedere College. His likes and dislikes of people were often based not on an emotional but on an intellectual judgement, a moral and ethical judgement of them and their beliefs. Asked by Marian Finucane if he liked Margaret Thatcher, he didn't answer. She asked him again. There was a long silence. Eventually he said: '*She* liked me.'

And there you have Garret. It was politically necessary that Mrs. Thatcher liked and trusted him in order for the

Anglo-Irish Agreement to come into being. But he couldn't bring himself to say in return that he liked someone of whose *laissez-faire* economic policies he would have profoundly disapproved.

But it was when he revealed that he had been to see his old and ailing rival, Charles Haughey, last October, that one was reminded what Titans they both were as compared with our present leaders. They'd been sparring partners since UCD days – Garret the upper middle-class Jesuit boy who frequented the Literary and Historical Society and the Law Society; who was the son of a Cumann na nGaedheal Foreign Minister and whose close friend was Declan Costello, son of a future Fine Gael Taoiseach. Charlie, in contrast, was the Brothers' boy from the Northside who concentrated pragmatically on the Commerce Society and the Students' Representative Council, and whose close friends were sons of Fianna Fáil Ministers, Harry Boland, Colm Traynor, Peadar Ward. Charlie had to rise through the social ranks fast, and he seized the political and accountancy route to money and power. Garret already had the social position and the confidence that went with it, confidence to start questioning established norms.

And what had they in common? Apart from being deeply ambitious, they were both high risk, even subversive figures, within their parties. Garret determinedly kidnapped conservative Fine Gael as a vehicle for his social democratic ambitions. Haughey played with fire by appealing to Fianna Fáil's irredentist Republicans in his bid for leadership.

They left us with problems but they also benefited us: FitzGerald forged a mature relationship between Dublin and London which has stood the test of time. Haughey, with the support of opposition leader Alan Dukes, was a late convert to the fiscal discipline which helped lay the foundation for our present prosperity.

But why do they seem so much bigger, more distinctive than our party leaders today? Well, largely because they *were* such challenging and divisive figures. They divided opinion inside their own parties and outside too. They were forged in a harder school and they were warriors, fighting the great set battles on Northern Ireland, on the economy, on contraception, abortion and divorce.

There is a policy consensus between all parties on so many of those issues now, and the partnership process is forging agreement even between employers and unions outside parliament. Prosperity oils the wheels of consensus and no one wants a high-risk leader. Enda Kenny at his most self-righteous and Pat Rabbitte at his most waspish are much of the time arguing only about who will better manage the loot of the boom.

So happy birthday, Garret, we miss you. But it is a lot quieter without you.

The Dog who didn't Bark

If there's one thing TDs can't stand, it's a blaze of good publicity for a constituency rival. When Dublin North-Central Independent, Finian McGrath, wowed the punters with his singing and guitar playing on RTÉ's 'You're a Star', there were angry mutterings about political bias. Eight straight nights starring on prime time television does make you a bit of a celebrity. But when Finian bumped into his fellow constituency deputy Richard Bruton the week after Michael McDowell's Goebbels outburst, it was Richard who was twinkling. 'This was my "You're a Star"' Finian,' giggled Richard. 'McDowell was my "You're a Star."'

Thanks to the Minister for Justice comparing him to Hitler's propaganda chief, Richard was portrayed all week as the angel his seraphic smile suggests he is. Michael McDowell, on the other hand, so fulfilled his mad dog caricature that when his wife went to the butchers on Friday, according to what she told Marian Finucane, the man behind her in the queue suggested she should stop feeding her husband red meat.

Bruton, though, was the dog who didn't bark and

that's always worth investigating. Because Bruton is deputy leader of Fine Gael, the man many people assumed would be leader. He's Finance spokesman but more important, he's Fine Gael's policy guru. He will be central to Fine Gael's election message, to whatever joint platform they create with Labour, and if they win, he'll be a senior minister, perhaps in Finance. When the poll figures show a continuing decline in Fianna Fáil support, everybody looks more closely at the opposition front bench. And before their eyes glaze over in despair, they focus on two bright spots: the optimistic trier who is Enda Kenny, and the policy workhorse who is Richard Bruton.

Bruton is a Jesuit boy who believes figures speak louder than words. He's an economist with a rare MPhil in economics from Oxford. He's cerebral, systematic, a believer in the power of rational argument and deeply uncomfortable with rhetoric. Neither does he like sensationalism. When he was appointed Health spokesman in 1990, following Ivan Yates, there was a worry that Richard might concentrate too much on the figures and the heavy stuff. So there was a front bench meeting where Ivan Yates was asked for advice about how to present health issues. Robust as ever, Ivan made it clear that there was no point in pussy-footing around; that you had to argue from the particular, to reflect people's misery and pain; that there had to be people, sick people, even very, very sick people at the centre of the case put forward by the opposition. Richard's face was a study in distaste. He was appalled. He doesn't operate like that.

In his two and a half years as Minister for Enterprise and Employment, he had a reputation for being fussy. A one page memo from a civil servant would be returned, it was said, with three pages of Richard's notes. He was accused of being indecisive, too ready to see all sides of the argument. But he did recognise, earlier than most, the need to train and upskill the workforce. He published an important White Paper on Human Resource Development and took a particular interest in the training of disadvantaged young people. And luckily for him, the first major employment surge of the economic boom – 150,000 new jobs – came in the years he was Minister.

He belongs to the 'Just Society' wing of Fine Gael. However, in government his economic training and his belief in the market led to some conflict with his Social Welfare colleague Proinsias de Rossa, and also with the unions over partnership. That conflict shows still in the policy differences Fianna Fáil are so happy to point up between Fine Gael and Labour – differences on privatisation of Aer Lingus and Great Southern Hotels, differences on benchmarking. But there's another legacy from his time as Minister, an important one politically. His super junior in the Department was Pat Rabbitte and they developed a close relationship. Bruton, who has no problems with ego, gave his junior space and recognition. The fact that Rabbitte is close both to the Fine Gael leader and his deputy will come in useful as pressures come on the putative alternative government.

And in case that angelic smile fools anybody, electorally Bruton is tough as nails and stubborn. For twenty-four years, he's survived in North Central, one of the most competitive constituencies in the country, once dominated by Charles Haughey. He does a Bertie on the constituency, nursing it in and out of election times, often doing door-to-door canvassing on an estate twice a week on the way home from the Dáil. Friends remember him refusing to stop to eat during election campaigns, eating broken biscuits from his pocket as he traipsed doggedly round the doorsteps.

He distrusts emotion, but it happens. I remember when his brother was unexpectedly elected Taoiseach in 1994, a surge of well-wishers swept John down the steps from the Dáil chamber to the cameras outside. Richard wasn't there. So I went up to the deserted Fine Gael rooms to find him in his office, fighting back the tears, overcome with delight for his brother. 'It's what he's always wanted,' he said simply. Years later, when John was removed and made his resignation announcement to the media, Richard was there at his shoulder.

Those who liked the Brute in Bruton find Richard dull. But he's loyal. And there are tough times coming when Fianna Fáil will focus in on Enda Kenny's biggest weakness – the perception that he's a lightweight with no grasp of the broad sweep of government policy. Kenny will need someone beside him who's loyal, heavyweight, and indefatigable.

He's got him.

Kings and Princes

When Albert Reynolds decided to challenge for the Fianna Fáil leadership, he voted no confidence in Charlie Haughey in autumn 1992. Driving down to Longford afterwards, he got a phone-call from Haughey, asking him to resign. 'No, I won't do that,' said Albert. 'I'll follow your own example.'

It was a neat political gibe, with more than a hint of menace behind it. Haughey would have to sack him, just as Haughey had forced Lynch to sack *him* in 1970. Haughey, in time, took out Lynch, just as Albert, in much less time, would take out Haughey.

They were both Finance Ministers, Haughey and Reynolds, and they both did for their leaders. It's an interesting relationship, that between Finance Minister and Prime Minister, because it's very often that between king and pretender.

It struck me particularly in one week in September 2004 with a fresh new finance minister here, and across the water, the glowering face of Gordon Brown, Britain's longest serving chancellor in modern times, thwarted yet again for the premiership he felt was his by right. And I wondered, will Brian Cowen's face look like this in seven years' time?

Finance is regarded as the crucible through which aspiring Taoisigh have to go. It wasn't always so. For historical reasons, WT Cosgrave and Dev skipped it. So did Seán Lemass, Liam Cosgrave, and Garret FitzGerald. But with politics dominated increasingly by economic matters, and less about the Civil War, a period in Finance is regarded as a necessary if not sufficient qualification for leadership.

It's a daunting department and it takes itself very seriously. 'The first thing I noticed about it,' says Albert Reynolds, 'is that the staff don't smile, it's all very solemn.' Finance is used to saying 'no' and any minister who wants his party to win elections has to push them to say 'yes' quite a lot. By the time history praises you for being a reforming and careful minister for Finance, you'll be history, too.

Finance ministers have more autonomy than any other member of cabinet but that too depends on the nature of the minister. The hapless Gene FitzGerald, Haughey's first Finance Minister, was little more than Haughey's cipher. Financial reporters still remember his first press conference where he pleaded with them, 'Don't be too hard on me now, lads.' At that time, once senior Finance people and the minister had signed off on the estimates, the senior officials would go straight over to brief the Taoiseach. Ruairí Quinn stopped that. Communication with the Taoiseach would be through him, nobody else. 'I'll brief the Taoiseach myself,' he insisted.

A Taoiseach can too easily undermine a Finance Minister and that's what's seen as having happened to Alan Dukes as Finance Minister in 1982. He announced that he wanted to bring the massive budget deficit he'd inherited from Fianna Fáil down to £750 million. Knowing that this involved cuts, the Labour Party protested and Garret FitzGerald rowed back publicly.

Ray McSharry, who didn't care what anybody thought of him, played tougher in his cutbacks in 1987. It worked but probably ensured that he would never be popular enough to become leader.

Bertie Ahern's relationship with Albert Reynolds was as near as Ireland comes to the Blair/Brown relationship. There was mistrust because, after all, Ahern had been Albert's rival for the leadership. But there was another factor. Albert saw himself as a successful businessman with a working knowledge of finance. It was he who pushed the tax amnesty, to which Ahern agreed only reluctantly. It was Albert's determination to keep up with the big boys in Europe which helped keep us trailing the soaring deutschmark for so long in the early nineties. Bertie made no secret of the fact that he was worried about the damage it was doing to the Irish economy.

Charlie McCreevy, however, was so determined to show his independence in his early years in Finance that even the Taoiseach occasionally had great difficulty in contacting him. 'He was like a man with his arms wrapped around a plate of spuds,' said one observer, 'guarding it against any greedy raiders.' But for all his supposed autonomy, McCreevy was ultimately Bertie's victim. He knew he needed to slow down spending in 2001 but Bertie, as ever, delayed the election for over a year and McCreevy had to keep the good times rolling until after the 2002 poll. Then he had to brake suddenly, and was seen cynically to be breaking just-made election promises. And with the economy picking up again, people punished Fianna Fáil in the subsequent local elections. It was mostly Bertie's fault, but Charlie had to go.

There's always a question of luck and of timing in these relationships. Haughey seized his chance in 1979, and Reynolds seized his in 1992. By the time Gordon Brown's moment comes, the British Labour Party's love affair with the voters may have faded. Maybe after the 2005 election, when Blair was battered by popular criticism of his stance on Iraq, and had begun to lose the will to go on – maybe that was the time to strike.

Brian Cowen has a lot going for him, including time. He became Finance Minister when he was only forty-four. When Albert brought him into the cabinet at the age of thirty-two, he introduced him to people on that first day as 'a future leader of Fianna Fáil'. He's lucky – from his first week in Finance, he's had the benefit of buoyant tax returns and overflowing coffers. He's a party loyalist, beloved by members and backbenchers alike. And he's supposed to be real tough.

But is he? If Bertie fails to move aside for him, will he wield the sword, will he kill the king? Only then, perhaps, will we know how tough he really is.

After Michael

As a young man, former Labour Leader Michael O'Leary
had TB. He studied for his Masters in Irish History on the
flat of his back in Sarsfield's Court Sanatorium above
Glanmire in Cork. His friend and fellow UCC graduate,
Barry Desmond, used to cycle up Watergrass Hill to the
sanatorium every weekend to see him. He'd deliver
books to him and collect other books which had to be
fumigated before being returned to the library.

O'Leary, fretting on his sick bed and cut off from the
world, used to write to all the different embassies for
information about their countries. The communist bloc
responded generously, and books and propaganda
leaflets began to pour in to Sarsfield's Court from the
Soviet Union and Eastern Europe to the consternation
of other patients and the nuns. After all, this was
Ireland in the fifties and when the rosary was said each
evening with the ward doors open and each ward
taking its turn to lead each new decade, they prayed
for the conversion of Russia, and for the soul of
Michael O'Leary. O'Leary was having none of it. As the
rosary droned on, he would take the red flannel TB

patients use to keep their chests warm, hoist it on top of a sweeping brush and march down the corridor singing 'The Red Flag'. There's no doubt about it – Micko had style.

And we were desperate for any bit of style, of colour. That's why we embraced President John F Kennedy like a young god when he burst on the scene in the sixties. Michael O'Leary, after his year at Colombia University in New York, adopted the Kennedy model. It was a little bit radical and very chic, eyes fixed on new horizons, winds-of-change-blowing-in-your-hair sort of stuff – and everything was urgent, urgent, urgent. Michael's Cork voice reflected it – in turn passionate, scathing, but always impatient. He was part of the 1960s new Labour Party intake – along with Barry Desmond and later Justin Keating, David Thornley, Conor Cruise O'Brien – all university-educated, internationalist, progressive, poised to be stars on the new stage opened by the Irish television service. They were a million miles from the traditional, drab, union-dominated Labour Party.

O'Leary always had a succession of beautiful women on his arm. They changed with dizzying frequency. Once, he arrived at a reception in the Department of Foreign Affairs where guests walked up the stairs to be received formally by the Minister. As O'Leary and his companion were announced, she turned to the toastmaster and said, 'No, that's not my name.' Michael had changed girlfriends since the guest list was drawn up. The then Minister, Paddy Hillery, enjoyed it all hugely.

O'Leary was a superb mimic. Colleagues said you never got to finish your lunch from laughing when he joined the table and his skill was that he didn't just mimic the voice; he mimicked the thought pattern as well. Once, when his fellow Cork man, Gene FitzGerald, was reluctantly and briefly Minister for Finance, O'Leary leaped up on the bar in Bowes of Fleet Street on budget night, and delivered the budget speech in a perfect imitation of Gene's hesitant Cork voice. The place was convulsed.

He may not have been a traditionalist, but he owed a lot to the unions. The Irish Transport and General Workers' Union (now SIPTU), for whom he worked, backed him politically. They ensured that he had an office and a secretary at Liberty Hall as a young TD – no other backbencher had that luxury. As Minister for Labour in the 1973–77 coalition, he was able to return the favour, introducing a whole body of legislation protecting workers' rights, including the Unfair Dismissals Act. Most of it, mind you, was demanded by Brussels. He dragged his feet, however, on introducing equal pay legislation, and only backed down in face of the howls of protest from women and the petitions signed by hundreds and thousands of us which forced Brussels to insist on implementation.

O'Leary's link with the unions also influenced his

definitive relationship within the Labour Party: his rivalry with Frank Cluskey. O'Leary was ITGWU. Cluskey belonged to the rival and Larkinite Federated Workers' Union of Ireland. Michael was Cork, while Cluskey was an unapologetic Dub. Michael had social pretensions. Cluskey had none. They baited one another right up through the seventies' coalition government. Eventually Cluskey beat O'Leary by one vote to take the Labour leadership after Brendan Corish retired in 1977. Waiting for Cluskey to address his very first party conference, a Labour aide was worried as to how he would handle it. 'Don't worry,' said Michael O'Leary brightly. 'He'll hold them in the hollow of his head.'

O'Leary could never concentrate on anything for very long – these days he might well be regarded as suffering from attention deficit disorder. But certainly, by the time he became party leader and joined Garret FitzGerald's 1982 coalition, one got the impression he was losing interest in politics. He did a television interview with me during the big snow of 1982 and with FitzGerald out of the country, he, as Tanaiste, was left in charge. We had dinner afterwards and suddenly he said to me: 'I'm bored.' 'But you can't be, Michael,' I protested. 'You're Tanaiste, Minister for Energy, leader of the Labour Party!' 'Yeah,' he said. 'And I'm bored.'

About ten months later, after he'd failed to persuade the Labour Party Conference to allow its TDs the freedom to decide on coalition, O'Leary gave up. He rang his colleague Barry Desmond to say he'd left the key of the Labour leader's office at the usher's desk in the hall of the Dáil. 'I'm going, Bar,' he said. 'I'm gone.'

And he was. He never really figured in Fine Gael or on the political stage ever again. And with him, for my 1960s generation at least, something disappeared – maybe something more of style than of substance: the jutting jaw, the toss of the head, the Cork voice that could sway a crowd and entertain a party. A reminder that we were all young once. And we're not any more.

Sunny Jim

It's not often that you want to cheer when watching a political interview. I did it once, though, watching ITV Weekend World's tenacious Brian Walden interviewing former Labour Prime Minister Jim Callaghan.

It was in the eighties. Labour in opposition was moving further to the left. Callaghan had obviously been invited to express his known opposition to Labour's new policy of disarming the UK's nuclear deterrent. Quickly it became obvious Callaghan was going to duck the issue. So ten minutes into an advertised thirty-minute interview, Brian Walden took a decision. 'Thank you for coming in,' he said to Callaghan. 'I don't think we need to waste any more of your time, my time, or more importantly, the viewers' time if you're going to refuse to answer the question. We'll end this interview now. Good day.' Up rolled the credits over an embarrassed Callaghan and the station switched to a filler.

It was as neat a dismissal as I've seen in political journalism and it says a lot about the late Jim Callaghan. Politically, Jim almost always failed to answer the question. Most of the time, Jim didn't even want to see the question asked.

Look at his record on two issues: UK trade union reform, and Northern Ireland. Jim Callaghan was welcomed as a saviour when he walked through the streets of Derry in August 1969. He'd sent in British troops to replace the hated RUC. A woman knelt and kissed his hand. He had cups of tea. He spoke with a megaphone out of Mrs Doherty's window. He gave an interview to RTÉ in the local bookie's shop. He was a great reassuring presence. Roy Jenkins was to say of him later that he never knew any politician with such a powerful personality ... and such little intellect.

And so it proved with Northern Ireland. After the initial proper decision to send in the troops, there was no attempt to take the next logical political step, the suspension of the Stormont government. It took two years and Bloody Sunday, and it was the Tories who did it. Indeed, until Tony Blair, no Labour government showed much readiness to think strategically about Northern Ireland at all.

Callaghan seemed to see the North primarily as a security matter. As Prime Minister, he appointed Roy Mason, the Secretary of State for Northern Ireland who more than any other saw Northern Ireland as a terrorist issue. Heading a minority government, Callaghan courted the votes of the Ulster Unionist Party and made a deal with them, one about which many senior labour figures were uneasy, to increase Northern Ireland representation in

Westminster. The SDLP warned this would increase unionist representation, which it did – but then Callaghan was often irritated by the SDLP. He once told Garret FitzGerald that he wasn't going to be led around by the nose by John Hume. As Prime Minister, he seemed to be merely drifting on the North and even admitted to Senator Ted Kennedy, quite unabashed, that he had no policy on Northern Ireland. His lack of interest cost him. On a vote of censure in 1979, his government fell by one vote and the sole SDLP MP, Gerry Fitt, usually an automatic ally, did not support him.

But where Callaghan spectacularly failed to answer the question was on the future of his own party. In 1966, Harold Wilson set about union reform because he knew the voting public was worried about increasingly militant unions and Labour's failure to curb them. His Employment Secretary, Barbara Castle, drew up 'In Place of Strife', a document which proposed pre-strike ballots, and a twenty-eight-day delay and fines for those who broke the rules. For Labour, this was a brave step. Facing down the unions required total cabinet solidarity. But old union organiser Jim Callaghan, then Home Secretary, broke ranks. He worked ceaselessly with union leaders to undermine the attempted reforms, eventually voting against his own government in a famous meeting of Labour's national executive. It was widely seen as a preparatory bid for leadership. 'A snake lurking in the grass,' was how Castle described him in her diaries.

When Brian Walden, then a Labour backbencher, argued with him that the union legislation was necessary and inevitable, Callaghan replied typically: 'OK, if it's so inevitable, let the Tories pass it. All I'm saying is that's it's not our issue.' It was an abdication of responsibility to his party and his country and, with poetic justice, widespread strikes brought his own premiership to a humiliating end in 1979. The Winter of Discontent swept Thatcher into power and kept her there. Whenever interviewers like me suggested to her that she was hard and uncaring, her blue eyes would widen and she would repeat as though chanting a mantra: 'Me uncaring? Remember the Winter of Discontent? Remember when we couldn't bury our dead? Remember when the streets piled up with rubbish?'

And people did remember, for a very long time. Margaret Thatcher shouldn't have been inevitable, but James Callaghan made her so.

INJURED PARTIES

Green Growth

Our butcher in Borris has some sharp political observations and he doesn't mind sharing them with his customers. 'You should be called the scary party,' he announced to the local Green Party representative in his queue one day, 'because what you do is go around scaring people.' Now Charlie gets away with saying stuff like that, because he's the best butcher in three counties.

But he hit on a real dilemma for the Greens. Do people vote for Prophets of Doom? Is the voter turned on by people in sackcloth and sandals constantly crying, 'Repent! Repent!'? I'm not saying the Greens haven't ever been right. They've been right so many times that it's well … scary. But how do you preach a message of restraint, of long-term sustainability, in a world which wants it all now?

Because we run away from the truth so easily. Remember the seventies – well now half of you don't, but I do. When oil prices jumped, we bought smaller cars or bicycles; we turned off the heating and bought wood-burning stoves; we insulated everything in sight. Now here we are thirty years later, wearing cotton t-shirts in our overheated houses and driving massive jeeps to the local supermarket. We've learned nothing.

And yet it was that time, back in the seventies, which bred a lot of our current crop of Greens. The oil crisis focussed people on the need to conserve, to move to sustainable growth which would not run down the Earth's resources. Many of them were inspired by Rachel Carson's book, *Silent Spring*, which warned of the consequences if we destroyed nature's balance and diversity. There was a TV series called the 'Good Life' with Felicity Kendall as the Greenest of sex symbols. Green was cool.

Now here we are again. Oil prices are hitting record levels. The fear of oil and coal and gas sources running out has resurrected interest in nuclear power, left on the back burner after Chernobyl. High oil prices, a new push for nuclear power, a Europe-wide concern about GM crops, and a worldwide concern about climate change create new opportunities for the Greens. So do the indications, confirmed by the by-elections in Kildare and Meath, that people are questioning the benefits of an economic growth which has left them leaving their kids into crèches at 6.30 in the morning and sitting in traffic into the city for hours every day.

But perhaps the most immediate issue which has left people thinking Green is waste. Many people are finding that domestic waste collection will cost them twice as much unless they cut back drastically.

In many areas, like mine, you pay more, the more you

put out – and rightly so. Suddenly, we're all sorting out paper, which is collected for free, and glass which goes to the bottle bank, and weekend conversations are dominated by composting and recycling and trips to the dump at Ballyogan. We're doing what the Greens told us we must do thirty years ago.

All of this must be fertile political ground for the party, but how do they benefit from it? Maybe this time round, they're conscious that scaring people isn't the best long-term strategy. 'Well, we're not going to jump up and down shouting, "I told you so",' says leader Trevor Sargent. 'We have more to be doing than writing ourselves a footnote in history. We're more interested in a vibrant economy which will pay for a good quality of life.' The most environmentally-conscious countries are also Europe's leading economies, he says, pointing to the Scandinavian countries and to Switzerland.

This generation of Greens is far from sandals and brown rice. They're the best-dressed sextet in parliament; they perform well; and in Greenspeak they are 'realos', meaning realistic, as opposed to 'unrealos'. Finance spokesman Dan Boyle quotes the great market economist, Adam Smith. 'Smith believed in a free market and so do we, a market where the full cost of goods is charged, including the cost to the environment of producing them.' We should stop subsidising polluters, he says. Greens, he says, are less materialistic than other parties, less obsessed with creating wealth than parties of the right, less obsessed with simply redistributing it, like parties of the left. There is a bigger picture.

They are not the lunatic political fringe party that Fianna Fáil and Michael McDowell like to present them as being, a caricature which will be drawn again and again as we get nearer to a general election. Given a few key issues – and a ban on incinerators would be only one of them – most of the parliamentary party will probably happily join a Rainbow Coalition. They're keen to get into government now.

It's not enough to remain a niche party, says their Dublin South Deputy Eamon Ryan, they have to grow. 'We must be careful not to become the Quakers of Irish politics, whom all the Catholics say are great. We actually need to become the Catholics.'

Well, if they want to grow, they need to major more on economic policy. Finance spokesman Dan Boyle has now started that process with tax proposals which include an increase in corporation tax to 15% as well as the imposition of a new carbon tax; with a list of the many tax breaks which they suggest should be terminated. They have also shown they can score against the government on the sleaze issue better than the other opposition parties. Their hands are clean and Trevor Sargent was the only opposition figure who managed to embarrass the Taoiseach in the Dáil about Minister Séamus Brennan and Chief Whip Tom Kitt famously losing their memories about political donations.

But the 'huggy' element still breaks through. Take the time Labour and Fine Gael wanted to use the last private members time before a holiday recess to have a motion of no confidence in Micheál Martin. It was over the then burning issue, the nursing homes pensions scandal. But the Greens refused. It was their time, they insisted, and they wanted to choose the issue.

And the issue was fur-farming.

In Search of the Republic

In the early seventies, and it was a time when people still asked such things, I was cornered by an old man at a Fianna Fáil Ard-Fheis . 'Are you sound,' he demanded, 'on the National Question?' Which national question did he mean, I asked sarcastically: the national level of unemployment, or of emigration, or of unequal pay for women? 'Och, you know well what I mean,' he said. And I did. He meant was I republican and did I vote Fianna Fáil?

Because, politically, Fianna Fáil owned the national question. They had successfully stolen it from other parties. Even to this day, Fine Gael still pulls its skirts back from any real association with Republicanism. In a recent Ard-Fheis speech, Enda Kenny claimed for his party the 'civilian legacy of Michael Collins' – none of Collins' nasty military stuff, you notice. And there you have the difference in the two parties. In Fianna Fáil, they shout 'Up the Republic'. In Fine Gael, they say 'Up the civilian legacy of Michael Collins'.

That's what happens when people steal your republican clothes. Except that Fianna Fáil has now become worried that the same thing will happen to them. Their

US consultants, Shrum, Devine and Donilon, advisers to the Democratic Party for generations, have warned that Fianna Fáil must beef up their republican credentials. The consultants' surveys have shown that there's fertile electoral ground out there for an unapologetic Republican party, and that Fianna Fáil have ceded too much ground in that area to Sinn Féin. The surveys reveal that Sinn Féin is winning voters among those who strongly disagree with Sinn Féin tax policies but who want a republican home, a home they feel they can't find any more in Fianna Fáil.

So no, it's no coincidence that our Bert has been polishing up the party's republican medals. Nothing our Bert does is ever a coincidence. That's why, at his party's Ard-Fheis, he announced the reinstatement of the traditional 1916 Easter Parade, involving the Irish Army marching past the GPO. 'The Irish people need to reclaim the spirit of 1916 which is not the property of those who have abused and debased the title of Republicanism,' he said.

That's why he's been highlighting the differences between Sinn Féin and Fianna Fáil on issues like tax and the economy and the EU rather than on any issue to do with Northern Ireland or Republicanism.

That's why he has emphasised his party's 32-county credentials by proposing recently that Northern MPs be given the right to speak in the Dáil twice a year, and by raising once in a while the prospect of a Fianna Fáil organisation in Northern Ireland.

It all makes perfect sense. Fianna Fáil has always glo-ried in its full title as the Republican Party, and the Taoiseach and the full parliamentary party attend annual republican ceremonies at Wolfe Tone's grave in Boden-stown and Arbour Hill – the only party to do Boden-stown other than Sinn Féin. It wraps itself in the national symbol, the national flag, and the national colours. The party logo is a green, white and orange harp and its web site is headed by a harp and a tricolour and is a sea of green, white and orange. Fine Gael's logo is a shooting star – a green one, mind you, but still reflecting more Walt Disney than Poblacht na hÉireann. So no competi-tion from Fine Gael on this front or from a Labour party led by Pat Rabbitte, who has a profound distaste for what he calls republican flag-waving and does none of it at his annual May commemoration of James Connolly at Arbour Hill.

So Bertie's republican crusade allows him a handy bit of product differentiation from the Opposition – all, that is, except Sinn Féin. The fact that the bombing has stopped in Northern Ireland and Sinn Féin and the IRA have at least promised to decommission the weapons and end the criminality presents him with two realities: first, Sinn Féin will be even more acceptable to a South-ern electorate; but second the absence of violence makes it respectable for constitutional republicans to proclaim their faith again.

Add to that the fact that recent economic success has

at last given us something to celebrate. For a very long time it wasn't just Northern Ireland, to use Charlie Haughey's phrase, which was a failed entity, but also this twenty-six-county Republic, with its unemployment and its tragic levels of emigration. There was very little to be patriotic about. One wonders whether this is why a revisionist view of history dominated in the difficult seventies and the awful eighties, one which questioned all the sacred cows of nationalism. Back then we had Joe Lee and Roy Foster. Now there's a new school of academic historians with a more unapologetic nationalist point of view: Cormac Ó Gradha, Mary Daly, Eunan O'Halpin, and more recently Diarmaid Ferriter. Prosperity has brought a new pride in who we are. Bertie may be on to something.

But the Bert feels that with the economy going so well, the government should be getting a better press. He blames unfriendly media coverage for the fall-off in his party's showing in the polls. It's known that he regards the media as his real opposition and feels that the broadsheet press, and RTÉ programmes like 'Morning Ireland', give the government an unfairly hard time. He bemoans constantly the loss of the Irish Press Group and feels that in international terms Fianna Fáil is almost unique in being a governing party without media friends. And that's how they see themselves. They are the government, but not the establishment. They wield power, but not influence. Though they've held office longer than any other party, they continue to consider themselves outsiders.

And that is part and parcel of Fianna Fáil's Republicanism. The party began among men on the run and still feels itself anti-establishment. It sees itself as of the people. It doesn't matter how often you point to the millionaire builders and brokers who support the party, or the excesses in the Fianna Fáil tent at the Galway Races, it still feels it belongs to the *gnáth-daoine*. It still gets the biggest bloc of their votes. Its TDs may have moved into the middle-class and the professions, but pretensions are discouraged. It's devoted to the cult of the ordinary. Fellas might enjoy Bach or Wagner, but country and western does fine in public, thank you very much.

Of the people and of the nation – it's a dual position the party has fought for and defended successfully for decades. That's why Sinn Féin gives it apoplexy. That's why, when Caoimhghín Ó Caoláin stands up to speak in the Dáil, the Fianna Fáilers talk loudly among themselves, while watching him carefully out of the side of their eyes. That's why, when he pursues some patriotic piety, they hiss like a dowager duchess whose pedigree has been questioned.

Nobody could outflank them, until now. Nobody dared to ask the question the old man put to me thirty years ago, the question Sinn Féin will now increasingly put to Fianna Fáil: 'But are you sound on the national question?'

At Sea with Sinn Féin

I remember going on a canvass once with Councillor Daithí Doolan, Sinn Féin's man in the Pearse Street area of Dublin. The issues were as you would expect: housing, welfare benefits, health. But as we moved along, he took a phone call which made him smile. It was a drama group from middle-class Sandymount, thanking him for helping them get a grant. Things were really changing for the party, he laughed, when you were getting calls like that.

I watched him and colleagues like Deputy Seán Crowe in Tallaght, going about a politician's humdrum daily business, and I remember thinking this is Sinn Féin embracing constitutional politics. This has to be good for all of us.

But now and then, something happens, which makes you feel, well, a bit seasick. On Joe Duffy's 'Liveline' programme, a young Dublin woman called Lisa came on the phone. She had joined the British Army seven years earlier and she wanted to know whether she was still to be regarded as what the Republican movement would call 'a legitimate target'. Ella O'Dwyer of Sinn Féin answered the question: 'She's part of the British Army, which is occupying the Six Counties, so obviously she's involved in a war. If she signs up to become a soldier in an army, then she's going to be a target.' Then Ella added: 'There's a cessation on, so she's not going to be shot while there is a cessation on.'

Now, funnily enough, I don't think the young soldier found that very reassuring and neither did I. Because behind Ella's lofty granting of a temporary reprieve to the young soldier, and indeed to the rest of us, was the reality we've all preferred to forget about, the IRA. They haven't gone away, you know.

It's easy to think they have, maybe because we so desperately want to believe it. But every so often, the veil slips. In the North, there's still a fog of unanswered questions about IRA/Sinn Féin involvement in the beating and murder of Robert McCartney and the intimidation of his family from the Short Strand area. PSNI chief Hugh Orde says the IRA was behind the Northern Bank robbery. He says they were behind the abduction of alleged dissident republican Bobby Tohill in Belfast. We still don't know.

What we do know is that the administration of justice is best left in the hands of the police. Indeed, here in the Republic, there is a dawning realisation among politicians of other parties that they and the gardaí ceded vital ground to Sinn Féin on the whole drugs issue.

One deputy has spoken to me regretfully of an incident in west Dublin, where local representatives, gardaí and residents stood by at a public meeting, while a member of the Republican movement interrogated an alleged drug pusher, who was then condemned to be removed from the area. This was work for the gardaí, not for anybody else. In this state, there should be one police force, and one army.

And it's ironic that Sinn Féin, who believe in nationalising almost everything else – state child care, state insurance company, state transport systems – make an exception when it comes to armies, or, as it's often put, their own private army.

Because this is the area, if you've noticed, that we're not allowed to ask about. When Martin McGuinness was questioned about the incident involving dissident republican Bobby Tohill, he used exactly the same dismissive phrase as Gerry Adams did. Politicians and the media rushing to judgement needed to 'catch themselves on', he said. He didn't think the Republican movement would be involved in anything which would undermine the peace process, he said. And he went on, 'The big question people have to ask themselves is: Do they value the Sinn Féin peace strategy and our contribution to the process, including our efforts to bring an end to physical force Republicanism? And if they don't, and prefer instead to return to the old agenda, then it's they who undermine the peace process.'

Now what does that mean? Is he saying that unless we

stop asking awkward questions and leave it to Sinn Féin to decide when the IRA closes up shop, well then we could have war again? And is that a friendly warning, or is it a threat?

And oh yes, I know that since September 2005, the IRA says it has decommissioned all arms and this has been verified by the Independent International Commission on Decommissioning. But does that mean that the army no longer exists, that it will no longer be engaged in illegal activities? And if anyone dares to raise a question about the Republican movement and illegal activities, will not Sinn Féin continue to cry that the peace process is being undermined? So for how long must we not ask questions? Until Sinn Féin has made historic gains in the forthcoming general election, winning votes from people too young to remember its campaign of violence, setting itself up as a handy coalition partner for Fianna Fáil? And all achieved with the army still intact?

And what will that mean for our democracy down here?

More than anything, what we wanted from the deal in Northern Ireland was a ceasefire, and that, generally speaking, is what we got. And we knew there'd be a price to be paid. But did we know that the price would be silence, our continuing silence, in order to preserve that ceasefire? Is the price paid yet? Will it ever be paid?

Kissing the Frog

We were always going to have to kiss the frog, you know. That was the deal. I used to have nightmares about that story when I was a kid. The princess loses her golden ball. She promises to have the frog as her friend and to kiss him if he fetches it. When he does, she runs away, but he pursues her and insists on sleeping on her pillow. And it was exactly that sort of I-don't-want-to-kiss-the-frog moment that we saw on a brilliant RTÉ 'Questions and Answers' one night as constitutional politicians from both sides of the border recoiled fastidiously from Sinn Féin's Mitchel McLoughlin, making it clear that they still don't accept that the Republican Movement has clean hands. As Pat Rabbitte described the self-appointed vigilantes, armed with hurleys and pickaxe handles, who administered justice in his Tallaght constituency, you could see Jeffrey Donaldson and Eamon Ó Cúiv nodding in agreement: you had to end not just paramilitarism, but also criminality.

That hasn't always been made clear and we here in the Republic have only very recently been made face the reality of what it's like living with a half-constitutional political party like Sinn Féin. Take the conviction for IRA membership of Deputy Aengus Ó Snodaigh's political associate and former secretary of Sinn Féin's South City branch, Niall Binead – a conviction against which he has appealed. Documentation on leading politicians was found at Binead's home, and he was arrested after an operation in which gardaí found four men inside a van. They also found a sledgehammer, two pickaxe handles, eight bags of ties, radios, a black balaclava, rubber gloves and a yellow fluorescent jacket with the word 'Garda' on it. In a Nissan car with false number-plates they found a blue flashing beacon, a Long Kesh cap, a stun gun, a canister of CS gas and a roll of black tape.

They're well used to this in Northern Ireland because they've been living with semi-democracy for some time. The Northern Bank raid, which PSNI Chief Hugh Orde insists is the work of the Provisional IRA, and the killing of Robert McCartney, are the most spectacular examples. But there are others: the long-established builder who made it clear he would not be doing any more developments in west Belfast because of the protection money he'd had to pay over: the raid on a white goods outlet in Belfast, which the International Monitoring Commission in one of its recent reports said was the responsibility of the IRA, whom it also blamed for a significant amount of smuggling. The head of the Assets Recovery Agency, Northern Ireland's version of the CAB, has told the SDLP that he believes 50% of fuel smuggling is done by, or for, the IRA.

But then that's all right, you see, because Gerry Adams says no member of the IRA could be a criminal. He said: 'You cannot be a criminal and a republican activist. You cannot be involved in any criminality and be involved in republican activism.' Does he mean that if a republican does it, then it's not a crime? Like the killing of Garda Jerry McCabe. It looked like a crime, but then they found out it had been authorised by the IRA so ipso facto suddenly it wasn't a crime.

So is that what's facing us in the Republic? And how will we feel about the sort of everyday threats Northerners face all the time: like some of the schools in nationalist areas who want to have the police talk to students about drugs, but who are warned off: like the areas of Derry where drunkenness and lawlessness on a Saturday night run unchecked because PSNI entry into the area brings on a riot; like the people who feel they can't speak up at residents' or community meetings against the wishes of the Sinn Féin activists?

The SDLP have been warning about this for years, that unchecked bullying in the back streets undermines democracy just as much as bombing campaigns in the city centres. They warned both governments that the ending of paramilitarism and criminality should be inextricably linked, not separated into two distinct issues as they were in the Hillsborough Agreement, into paragraphs 13 and 17.

As long ago as four years ago, Alex Attwood, SDLP

policing spokesperson, came down to Dublin to warn the Garda Commissioner and the head of the Criminal Assets Bureau that even if you ended paramilitary activities, but not criminality, you were asking for trouble. With Sinn Féin in government in the North, and perhaps holding the balance of power in the South, how confident could anybody be that the full force of the law would be brought to bear on criminals? How many of us wonder even now whether the full force of the law North and South is being muzzled in the interests of finding a political agreement?

There was always going to be pain for the gain in this agreement and we in the booming Republic have grown unused to pain. We should perhaps look to the Germans and see what they have paid and still pay for their new Germany, and realise that the road to a new Ireland is going to be hard and rocky and costly. And if the price is the dilution of our democracy, the rule of the pickaxe handle and the baseball bat in whole areas of our Republic, have we any right to pay it?

Maybe Ian Paisley, by holding up the process, and allowing us to have this debate, has done us all a favour. Because we need to ask ourselves whether the republican frog, once kissed, will turn out to be a prince, or whether he'll stay the same old frog, dragging us all down into the slime with him.

A Touch of Class

In the British Labour party, they do it with mugs. That's how middle-class or even upper-class Labour Ministers try to mix it with the masses. When I interviewed Shirley Williams in 1974, she offered me a china cup but pointed out proudly that she took *her* tea in a mug. Tony Benn plonked his beside my tape-recorder and, in case I didn't get the message, declared in ringing tones: 'I never go anywhere without my trusty tea mug.' Tony Blair still uses his, coming outside Number 10 in shirtsleeves to announce the birth of his son Leo, and grasping as his badge of proletarianism the inevitable mug of tea.

It's a dilemma for Labour Party leaders, this need to balance your two constituencies: the middle-class liberals and the working-class trade unionists. That's why the British Labour toffs use mugs and why the middle-class boys in the Irish Labour Party, like Ruairí Quinn, are the ones who most feel the need to address us all as 'Comrades'. For Labour in this country, there are many issues on which both those constituencies agree. But there are many on which they clash. And the question of migrant workers is one of them.

There are others. On contraception and divorce, working-class areas were often more conservative than middle-class areas. A similar issue is arising right now over the whole question of same sex marriages. Is Labour going to take the classic liberal line and alienate some of its more traditional vote?

The immigrant issue has always been politically difficult for the party, from the Refugees Act, introduced by the Rainbow coalition in 1996, to the referendum on Citizenship on which Labour, of the main parties, took what many people saw as a brave but lonely stance, a stance supported by only 17% of those who voted. Pat Rabbitte may well ask where the middle-class liberals who should have been supporting him went on that day.

As one Labour supporter put it to me this week: 'Middle-class liberals are all in favour of multiculturalism, but the nearest they come to it is their local Indian restaurant, or the Filipino who cleans their house, or the hardworking Polish mechanic who does their car repairs for nothing in jig-time.' Another woman pointed out: 'When you cross the Liffey to Dublin South-east or Dún Laoghaire, the immigrant issue no longer exists.' The middle class, she said, actually benefits from the influx of migrant workers. They benefit either as employers, or as users of cheaper services. It is the working class who compete with migrant workers for jobs, and who compete with asylum-seekers for public housing.

Still, there were many Labour people, veterans of the

liberal leadership of Dick Spring and Ruairí Quinn, veterans of the great liberal battles on divorce and abortion, on women's rights, on citizenship rights, whose hearts sank when they read Pat Rabbitte's comments in *The Irish Times* about the possible introduction of work permits for some non-national labour even from the European Union, and who blanched at his glib warning: 'There are forty million or so Poles after all, so it is an issue we have to look at.' He had many phone-calls from senior party figures, furious at what they called his sloppy language. Others in the party were angry that he even mentioned the possibility of work permits since it turns out it was only an empty threat. Did it suit him to sound more negative about migrant workers than he actually was, they wondered? He had a stormy parliamentary party meeting to get through before the issue was put in a context which satisfied them. That context was the protection of all workers' rights contained in the party's policy document 'A Fair place to work and live'. It stressed, among other things, the need to increase the state's Labour Inspectorate, to tackle bogus subcontractors and the bogus self-employed, and to extend equality legislation to cover those in domestic service. It also called for change in the controversial EU Services Directive which would allow workers here to be employed under conditions acceptable in their country of origin.

But the issue has revealed another fault-line within the

party, the divide between liberal old Labour and the pragmatic Stalinists of Democratic Left, the ones who now lead the party. The Democratic Left comes from a tradition which had little time for bleeding heart liberals. Many of the old Democratic Left people were impatient with Labour's liberal stance in the Citizenship referendum. 'It was a trap set by the PDs and Fianna Fáil. The liberals in the party locked onto it without asking was it a worm or a sardine,' said one scornfully. 'It lost us 3% in the local elections.'

The focus groups used under Pat Rabbitte have revealed to the party again and again that immigration plays big with voters. The trade unions have long been concerned about displacement of workers. But it was probably when he looked around him at the size of the Irish Ferries protest march that Rabbitte fully realised the strength of the issue. It's no coincidence that the party's poll rating immediately rose. And his critics in the party aren't sure whether that makes them feel sick or happy. 'It ain't a mortal sin to be popular, you know,' admitted one, uneasily.

Rabbitte's liberal record across a range of issues is clear, much clearer than most of those on the government side who have criticised him. But he probably has one chance of getting back into government and this is it. Old Stalinists don't mess when it comes to power. Compromises may be made which change the nature of the party.

Labour has always liked to think of itself as generous and outward-looking, welcoming all comers, the party which challenged many of the institutions which kept this country insular. That's why many people tradition-ally supported it. Will they now have to look elsewhere?

Keep your Eye on the Rabbitte

If you read your Anthony Trollope – and I'm sure the Labour Leader, an English graduate, has read his – then you'll recognise Pat Rabbitte's parliamentary style. It's straight from the Pallisers, or from 'The Way We Live Now', from the mid-Victorian glory days of the House of Commons. It's elegant, rhetorical, commanding, superior, and it really gets up Bertie's nose.

Because The Bert really doesn't like clever clogs. Fellas who put other fellas down have never played big in Drumcondra. Rabbitte's references to Bertie as our first non-English-speaking Taoiseach don't help – nor does the fact that Rabbitte, despite his west of Ireland accent, has adopted a style that we see every day at Westminster. Superiority is bad enough, but British-style superiority is something else.

So our Bert gets his own back. Before Christmas, we had the strategic leak of a Fianna Fáil secret document suggesting growing mutiny in the Labour Party at Pat Rabbitte's refusal to go into government with Fianna Fáil. Then, the weekend before Valentine's Day, Bertie strikes again, love-bombing the Labour Party, hinting at a future in government. It's about the third time he's done it in the space of three months. And he doesn't do it only to annoy. It's a well-thought-out strategy that he used to some effect coming up to the last election. Constant Fianna Fáil hints to Labour about a coalition kept Labour from making a pre-election pact with Fine Gael. It kept Labour attention focussed not on the election, but on what was going to happen after it.

This time, however, Bertie has a number of targets. First on his list is transfers – Fianna Fáil could do with Labour transfers, particularly in Dublin. Second, the trade union movement. He knows that many of the unions, who have traditionally had a better relationship with Fianna Fáil than the Labour Party, would be happy with a coalition. Fianna Fáil gets a massive working-class vote and Bertie's links with the union movement are strong and go back a long way. Third, talk of coalition with Labour keeps the PDs on their toes. But fourthly, his aim is to run interference on the Labour/Fine Gael partnership. He knows that many of the old Labour Party, people like Brendan Howlin and Michael D Higgins and Ruairí Quinn, were perfectly happy in government with Fianna Fáil and that there is an 'old Labour' suspicion of the new Democratic Left rule in the party which is easily exploited. If Bertie can create internal dissent in Labour, it will weaken the joint opposition front against the government.

Because many of the old Labourites will point out that

they come up against an ideological wall much faster with Fine Gael than they do with Fianna Fáil. Fine Gael's Christian Democrat conservatism caused them major problems in the eighties when there were major clashes between Dick Spring and Bruton and Dukes over cuts in spending, over whether Dublin Gas was to remain in private hands. There were no such clashes when they were in government with Fianna Fáil. Fianna Fáil recognised Labour's need to bring its own constituency with it, because Fianna Fáil shared that very same constituency.

'If your motivation in politics is to change society, Labour can do that much more effectively with Fianna Fáil,' said one Labour deputy who had served in cabinet with Fianna Fáil. 'If we had been in government with Fianna Fáil since 1997, we would now have a left-of-centre society in this country in terms of infrastructure.'

There must be many people in the Labour Party who look back to the fateful day in 1994 when Dick Spring pulled out of government with Fianna Fáil and ask themselves why. Why, when they could have got rid of Albert Reynolds and gone into government with the most pro-Labour leader Fianna Fáil could have chosen, Bertie Ahern, did Labour turn away? By doing so, they lost the possibility of continuing in government with Fianna Fáil throughout the fattest years of the boom, of influencing the social agenda so that the fruits of prosperity reached those who needed help most, of being in power at the only time in our history when we could afford to make aspirations a reality.

For those involved in the negotiations at the time, the sudden change of partners was dizzying. Ruairí Quinn had negotiated a return to government under Bertie Ahern, only to see that deal collapse. Within days he was negotiating instead with Fine Gael and Democratic Left.

At two in the morning Quinn was ticking off items which had been agreed, when they came to one where Richard Bruton of Fine Gael, ever polite, intervened and said, 'No, that hasn't been agreed.' Quinn, exhausted, lost the head. 'For Heaven's sake, don't you remember? We hammered it all out. Of course it's been agreed!' He was working himself up into a fine old lather when his colleague, Brendan Howlin, kicked him sharply on the ankle. 'No. That's what we agreed with Fianna Fáil, remember?' he whispered. 'Not with this lot'.

There will always be those in the party who say the collapse of the deal with Fianna Fáil was an historic opportunity missed. There will be others who say no one could then have predicted the boom. Not true. The economy had started to pick up after the exchange rate crisis in early 1993. By the end of 1994, real GDP growth was running at 6.1%. The growth in employment for the year to April 1994 was already over 3% and by the following April was 5%. The signs were already there.

What is worth noting, however, is that not everybody in Fianna Fáil was one hundred per cent behind the renewal of the coalition with Labour in 1994. Noel Dempsey is said to have resisted it mightily, leading a country-and-western group which included Máire Geoghegan-Quinn, Michael Smith, and may even have included Albert-Reynolds loyalist, Brian Cowen.

By now, however, Cowen would have no problem sitting in government with Labour. His last budget reflected much of the Labour agenda, particularly the ending of many tax breaks, the increase in social welfare and the emphasis on childcare.

For Bertie, every single ounce of whose energy is now focussed on winning a third term in office, Rabbitte's open hostility and contempt – but more importantly his strategic stance against Fianna Fáil – are major obstacles. The Taoiseach knows a post-election coalition with Labour would achieve two sweet aims: a confirmation of the leftward swing Bertie has already calculated will please the voters; and the inevitable resignation of Mr Pat Rabbitte.

This isn't a love-bomb. This is war.

VOTE FOR ME!

Day of Reckoning

There's a moment of quiet drama which happens about every four or five years or so. You walk into an empty school or local hall, you take a piece of paper, and you make your mark on it. And as you leave, you're meeting women struggling in with prams; older people hobbling in on crutches; fellows who have parked the lorry outside to hop in for a minute. And all around the country on that day, something extraordinary is going on: for that whole day, the country is in the hands of the people, of the voters. For that whole day at least, democracy is happening.

And it still moves me. Despite the fall off in voting, and increasing cynicism about politics, I still find Election Day exciting, uplifting. I stand and I watch people come and go from the polling station, knowing that currents are shifting, power may be changing as the people will it, and nobody will thwart them.

Election Day is the real drama, but the count is dramatic too, and before the government has a chance to take its benighted electronic machines out of storage and foist them on us again, I thought I'd remember some of the great marathon counts.

The one dear to my own heart was in Carlow-Kilkenny, June 1981. In a battle for the last seat, it was high noon between the two Fianna Fáil candidates: Jim Gibbons who had given evidence against Charles Haughey in the Arms Trial and had been thrown out of cabinet by Haughey, and Tom Nolan, Haughey loyalist and now Minister for Labour. To add to the rivalry, Gibbons came from County Kilkenny and Nolan from County Carlow and when Nolan was declared the winner by twenty-one votes, Gibbons called for a recount.

When the rechecking started on Monday, there were so few votes between the candidates that fellows were called in with rulers to measure the length of a No. 1 on a ballot paper, so they could be sure there was more of the 1 opposite one candidate's name than another. On the Tuesday, the Returning Officer brought both candidates into the room at the back to search for the Muckalee box from Kilkenny – potentially good news for Gibbons. When found, however, it was properly empty, but then Tom Nolan asked for a search of all the Carlow boxes and, lo and behold, one was found with 171 votes in it. It was from Rahanna, at the foot of Mount Leinster, and when that was announced, the Nolan supporters didn't even wait for the recount. They high-tailed it to Rahanna, a tiny village with two pubs. They drank Osborne's dry and then proceeded to do the same in Coady's.

The celebrations overcame caution for one Nolan supporter who had taken sick leave from the Carlow Sugar Factory to canvass. He said he had a bad back, but when he appeared on the front page of a daily paper, carrying Nolan on his shoulders from the count-centre, he was in trouble. Deputy MJ Nolan, then a youngster, has vivid memories of that turbulent election period of the early eighties. His father lost the seat back to Jim Gibbons only seven months later in February 1982, and MJ took the seat back from Jim Gibbons in November 1982.

But the longest count, perhaps the longest in the history of the state, was in 1997, the Dublin South Central count in the RDS. It went on for twelve days, with 120 hours counting. The stand-off was between Ben Briscoe of Fianna Fáil and Eric Byrne, then of Democratic Left, now a councillor with the Labour Party. The result mattered. If Byrne won, there was the possibility of a Fine Gael-led rainbow coalition. But if Briscoe won, then Fianna Fáil would make up a coalition with the PDs, supported by independents. After three full recounts, it came down to Briscoe being five votes ahead. Two further suspect votes were found, but three would have been needed to have stopped the declaration for Briscoe, so Byrne conceded defeat. It was exhausting. Tied to their twenty-four tables, the counters had made up a banner: 'Release the RDS 24'. Byrne said he and his supporters had camped there like Bedouin, and that it was even worse for them than for him, because they'd given up all their annual leave to canvass and now they didn't even have a result.

For Labour's Councillor Nicky Kelly in Wicklow in 2002, the count went on over two weekends with a post-ponement during the week because the hall wasn't available. There were three recounts before Independent Mildred Fox was declared the winner. Mildred had supported the government, so Fianna Fáil turned out in force for her and watching the Fianna Fáil veterans, says Kelly, was an education in itself. Kelly says he had a lot of amateur checkers, but they were experts by the end of that count. It was tiring, but it was democracy in action, declares Kelly. There was a proper paper trail to follow. And at least candidates had a chance to compose themselves about the result before facing the public.

There was no such chance for Joan Burton, whose Dublin West constituency was electronically counted in 2002. She remembers a hot steamy June night in that new-built shrine to the Celtic Tiger, Dublin City West Hotel, with drink from the bar flowing around the count. Suddenly the Returning Officer made a move and there was a stampede forward in which Joan and other candidates were left behind.

When she finally fought her way to the front to ask what had happened, she was told by one of the counting staff, 'Oh, didn't you know? They've just announced it. You've won.' All over, just like that. So much for build-up, so much for drama.

And it matters that politics retains the sense of theatre that keeps it interesting for the ordinary citizen. Sure, there are other arguments against the electronic voting system, particularly the lack of a proper paper trail of evidence to persuade the voter the process is fair.

But drama matters too, and the more machine-led and clinical a process becomes, the less interesting it is. And the less people will participate. And then the danger is that the day of reckoning, the day when the citizens in schools and halls all around the country finally have their say and cast their vote, the democratic miracle itself, will disappear.

Brigadoon

It was like a Brigadoon appearing out of the mists, the world as it once was and as Fine Gael would dearly like it to be again. Here were those long-lost party supporters – prosperous red-faced farmers with hats and stout sticks, goodly farm wives in flowered dresses and aprons – all setting out their stalls with home-made cheeses and prize pigs and steam-powered tractors and everybody, but everybody, seemed to be voting Fine Gael.

And into this dream world at Dunderry County Fair stepped Fine Gael European election candidate, Mairead McGuinness, all in cream, a veritable milk-maid on this vintage celebrity farm. It was home territory in County Meath for the *Farming Independent* editor and RTÉ Presenter of 'Ear to the Ground', and she was taking a light hand with the canvassing, dawdling through the afternoon crowd. 'Give us a bite of your choc-ice,' she said to a prospective voter. He did. The vote went without saying.

One woman worried about God being left out of the European constitution but most people wanted to tell her how much they liked her on TV. There was a man with a green wig who kept popping up wanting to sell her his prize-winning sheep; and another man who said he'd vote for her if she bought his heifers; and another man who liked her so much he wanted to pin the red rosette for best organic pigs onto her chest.

She's a country girl who lives on a farm herself so she took it all with weary good humour. The country men keep telling her she looks thinner than she does on television and then, she says ruefully, they take the opportunity to give her a squeeze just to check. It happened even as she sat on a vintage tractor to have her picture taken with the local election candidates. From nowhere, a horny hand sneaked around her waist and grabbed her. 'Did he leave his big fingerprints on me suit?' wailed Mairead. He didn't.

But there is no end to the things a budding politician has to endure. As a line of solemn faced traditional musicians played, she got pulled onto the dance-floor by a partner who pushed her into the Meath equivalent of a clog-dance. As the other couples fled for safety, she stomped her best and then escaped to the microphone to ask briefly for a few votes. But it wasn't over yet. Retreating from an old-time waltz, she bumped into Paddy Wall, formerly of the Food Safety Authority. 'You deserve to win,' Paddy called after her gallantly and then spoiled it all by whacking her rump soundly with his stick as though she were a prize heifer.

She was a good candidate for Fine Gael, so good that running-mate and sitting MEP Avril Doyle's nose was slightly out of joint.

The two women were coolly polite. Their style could hardly have been more different – Mairead down home and easy, Avril more Lady Bracknell, though a very sexy Lady Bracknell. Mairead's camp complained about Avril's presence up in Mairead's area when the party leader was on tour there – the local candidate is usually allowed to monopolise the publicity. Avril looked put out that Mairead was placed beside the leader for the European campaign launch and absented herself from the subsequent photo shoot.

The feeling in the party was that Avril shouldn't have shown she cared. She is the more experienced player with a good junior ministerial record at the Office of Public Works helping to refurbish Dublin Castle. She's been leader of the Irish delegation of the European Parliament's biggest grouping. But in the end, the rivalry between the two big-hitters played well in the press, swept most of the other Leinster constituency coverage off the page, and Fine Gael's gamble paid off: they both got elected with Mairead pulling in massive support – one out of every four first preference votes.

And you could have guessed it all back in Dunderry. Even the local Fianna Fáil canvasser welcomed Mairead like a long-lost friend. 'I'm getting the ears roasted off me here,' he confessed to her ruefully. But before she left, they did manage to find a Fianna Fáil voter, a Dev supporter, as they put it quaintly. He was the son-in-law of the Fair's resident matchmaker 'Will you give me a scratch?' Mairead asked him. 'Well, I won't forget you anyway,' said the Dev man carefully and then his wife pushed him aside. 'Don't worry,' she said stoutly, 'I'll be voting for you.' And all was well with the world again. The Fine Gael sun shone brightly over Brigadoon.

The Sorcerer's Apprentice

Royston Brady regards himself as Bertie's political son, no doubt about it. As we whirled through Drumcondra on Royston's European election canvass one Saturday, he peered across anxiously at Bertie's constituency centre, St Luke's. 'It's all right. The car is there and the light is on,' said Royston, relieved and happy. Bertie was in his office and all was well with the world.

Because they are two of a kind – the Sorcerer and the Sorcerer's apprentice. Not that our Bert is as flash as then Lord Mayor and European candidate, Royston Brady, though he does go to the opening of an envelope and he does get his picture in magazines like *VIP* and *Hello*, and he does believe in the political imperative of shaking hands a lot – 'a few hundred a day' is Royston's formula.

No, the real magic lesson learned from Bertie is to be the anti-government government candidate, to learn the masterly use, as one Fianna Fáil sage put it, of the third-person plural. When Bertie wants to distance himself from his own government, he refers to them as 'they'. Royston does the same. When a man at the Omnipark Shopping Centre in Santry complained about clampers,

154

Royston, the Lord Mayor whose own council authorised the clamping, agreed, saying it had started off as a good thing but was now losing focus. When a woman complained to him that the government had failed to tackle the consultants' hold over the health service, and another complained about the money wasted on the constant digging and re-digging up of roads, Royston agreed – Royston whose own government is in charge of reforming the health service, and whose own council authorises the digging up of the roads!

It's spellbinding to watch – now you see the government, now you don't. When a woman who told him she was going to protest outside the Dáil because his government had failed to build new premises for her children's school, Scoil Columbcille, Royston didn't miss a beat. 'And come around after the protest for a cup of coffee in the Mansion House. And how many of you are there? Bring the others,' said Royston. With one hand he's sympathising with people about what THEY, the government, are doing; with another he's talking down details of people's complaints because they know he has power and has access to power.

He's agin the government on foreign policy, too. He says his attitude towards the US invasion of Iraq and the US military's use of Shannon had been changed by the revelations about the behaviour of US troops. 'I wouldn't be chasing out to welcome George Bush when he comes,' said the Lord Mayor of Dublin.

He's the anti-authority authority figure: the Lord Mayor who called members of his own council 'clowns' and a 'waste of space'; who said Michael McDowell, the Justice Minister was an 'arrogant bully'. And it's not a bad tactic when the government is facing a cross electorate. There were those who cheered him for it all around the Northside on Saturday. 'You tell it like it is!' called out one man. But in a day when the issue of Europe came up only once, there were just as many who refused his leaflet, who pointedly returned it to him, and a few who told him that his government was a waste of time. One woman said she'd be voting for the other Fianna Fáil candidate, Deputy Eoin Ryan.

And indeed, Eoin was his real opposition. There was only one seat in Dublin for Fianna Fáil and the choice is between Royston in the North who has no political experience but lots of chutzpah and Eoin Ryan in the South, for twelve years deputy for Dublin South East and former Junior Minister who had responsibility for the National Drugs Strategy and oversaw the state's largest investment plan to fight drugs. Ryan is part of the Fianna Fáil aristocracy – son of senior figure, Senator Eoin Ryan, who stood out against Charles Haughey, and grandson veteran republican, Jim Ryan, former Fianna Fáil Minister for Finance. Unlike Royston, who wasn't ready to name the accession countries to the EU when asked on a radio quiz, Ryan is pitching for the informed vote on Europe, particularly in the business community.

But Royston had the publicity advantage of being Lord Mayor of Dublin, which may be the reason Ryan objected to a division of the constituency, knowing that Royston as Mayor could turn up wherever he liked. So the battle of the posters began. Some roads had Eoin posters and double posters of both candidates, Eoin on top, Royston on the bottom. Other roads had Royston posters, and double posters, with Royston on top and Eoin on the bottom. Eoin's had the 'o' picked out in European stars, and said 'Europe needs experience'. Royston's had the stars making a misty halo around Royston's head, and came in three different versions saying 'Energy', 'Drive', 'Commitment'. It was a battle between experience and neck, and who's to say who would have won it if Royston hadn't blundered into that strange controversy over his father's alleged abduction at the time of the Dublin bombings?

Imagination was always Royston's strongest brief. As we left the Oscar Traynor Complex in Coolock, where he'd been presenting cups to the footballers, we passed some young players from a visiting Belgian team. 'Are you the King of Ireland?' they called after Royston, resplendent in his golden chain. Smiling, Royston demurred. But there was a thoughtful look on his face. Now what if there *were* an election for the King of Ireland ...?

Old Soldiers

'Are you with the Gerry Adams crowd?' a big woman asked Proinsias de Rossa outside Superquinn in Finglas. 'No, I was never with the Gerry Adams crowd,' replied Proinsias grimly.

I can see why she got confused. The same beard, the same grizzled look, the same connections with a revolutionary past. Except that Proinsias is at a different stage of evolution. He was jailed as a youngster for being a member of the republican youth organisation, Fianna na hÉireann, but rejected violence over thirty years ago. Although the Official IRA continued to exist after the republican split, Proinsias and others kept travelling away from it until they arrived in the Labour Party. Still, something hangs about him of those years in the wilderness. He's a loner, cool, always alert to danger. Nothing surprises him, nothing shocks him. He's seen it all before.

'Where were ya for the last five years, ya bastard ya?' shouted a man, driving past on Barry Green in Finglas. 'In Brussels,' answered Proinsias. He's matter of fact. He doesn't slap backs, or pretend he can solve everyone's local problem. When people ask about housing, or louts on noisy motorbikes, he hands them on to the local councillor or to local TD, Róisín Shortall. 'I'm running for Europe,' he says firmly.

The issue he doesn't pass on – and it comes up all the time – is immigrants.'There are people coming in here and they don't even know where Ireland is on the map and they are getting grants,' said a woman outside the supermarket. 'And look how well they're dressed!' Another woman in black was finding it hard to make up her mind about the citizenship referendum. 'You can't have people rushing in here,' she said, slowly. 'I mean, we've only just got a bit of prosperity ourselves!' It was a difficult issue, agreed Proinsias, and that was why Labour was saying vote 'No'. We needed more time to look at the issues, he said.

At the Tesco shopping centre in Finglas South, a blonde woman in a lilac top is giving out about immigrant workers. Economists and employers will point out that immigrants have added greatly to the skills base of the economy and have reduced wage inflation, but she complained that they worked for less than their Irish counterparts. 'Why can these foreigners come in and charge six euros an hour?' After all, her son trained for four years, she argued. Proinsias agreed that some of the rates given to immigrant workers were illegal, but, he pointed out afterwards, people battling for scarce resources will always find a scapegoat to blame if they lose out. It used to be single mothers. Now it's immigrants.

This is home country for Proinsias. He keeps coming across people who knew his father, or his mother, or who knew him as a boy. He gets a chance to tell one woman what he's done for women in Europe, how he's worked to improve the work-life balance for people with families. He hands out thumbnail-sized books about European rights and the kids love them. 'Oh animal!' says one delighted boy with a crew cut, and calls over all his friends.

Proinsias also comes across people who benefited from his time as Minister for Social Welfare. One woman compliments him on setting up MABS, the Money Advice and Budgetary Service, and says it helped curb the money-lenders. Others remember the more than 260 million pounds he handed out in backdated social welfare equality payments to married women.

But as he wanders along, he seems strangely detached from the Labour women in their red 'Vote de Rossa' overalls. Being in Europe isolates him a bit, but there's also the fact that he was initially less enthusiastic about joining the party than his colleague, Pat Rabbitte. So remembering the tortuous road he's travelled, what's left of what he started out with?

He *was* republican and anti-partitionist – that's gone.

He *was* anti-EU and fought against EU referendums, including Maastricht. That's gone. He's now so enthusiastically in favour of closer union that he signed a document with other socialist MEPs in 2001 called 'A New Federalism'. It envisaged the EU Commission as the new government of Europe; with the Commission President as Prime Minister; and the head of the Council of Ministers as President – a new European entity supported by a military capacity. It seemed far stronger than the Labour Party's own position and was driven by a need to find a counterbalance to the US.

And maybe that's what remains of de Rossa, the old revolutionary, the old Stalinist – the determination that there will be some countervailing power in the world to the capitalist might of the United States. Moscow can no longer provide it, but maybe Europe can, and, for the moment, Proinsias de Rossa is there to ensure that it does.

Novo Provo

'The men of 1916 didn't die for that,' declared Joe in the Carnlough Road area of Cabra West. He thought Sinn Féin was wrong to be urging a 'No' vote in the citizenship referendum. 'We can't afford to have people coming in here,' said Joe. 'There is a small enough cake and there are too many people trying to eat from it.' Mary Lou McDonald held her ground. 'The men of 1916 believed in equality and this is about two babies born here in the same hospital having the same rights,' she said. 'No. That bit was put into the constitution to facilitate nationalists in the North, not to facilitate people from Nigeria or Kosovo,' said Joe. 'You are going to lose support. I'm giving you a bit of friendly advice. You keep your mouth shut about it.'

He was going to vote for her though, so Mary Lou and Joe agreed to disagree and she moved on. The heels of her suede boots are worn down with walking. This has been a long campaign and Sinn Féin has been well prepared for it with armies of helpers out. They've been on the canvass here for local and European elections since January – twice a week and on Saturdays, with teams of fourteen.

Mary Lou is the new Sinn Féin, soft around the edges, attractive, warm and very relaxed. She's thirty-seven with two very small children. A Trinity graduate and former researcher with the Institute for European Affairs, she's a middle-class girl with the middle Dublin accent of her generation – she sounds a bit like 'Prime Time's' Miriam O'Callaghan. It's hard to demonise Mary Lou. Even if the PDs were to dress her in sniper-at-work t-shirts and *ttocfaidh-ár-lá* badges, they wouldn't sit easily on her. She looks at home in her light blue linen jacket. She came from a Fianna Fáil family, but they weren't put out when she left Fianna Fáil to join Sinn Féin, she said. Her sister came with her. And yes, she would have been ready to join even before a ceasefire was declared by Republicans, she said.

She lets the locals lead on the canvass. 'I'm waiting to be told what to do,' she says simply. And the party shepherds her carefully into areas of strong support. Unlike other parties who go to shopping centres and public places, Sinn Féin is canvassing more from door-to-door, and having private meetings with community groups. It's almost as though they don't want to risk public confrontations. On Friday we were around Whitefriars Street with Daithí Doolan. Last night it was Cabra – the stronghold of Sinn Féin Councillor Nicky Kehoe. 'Our supporters expect us to come to the door,' said Mary Lou.

Anyhow in Cabra, people like to stay at home. 'I've

been decentralised three times and I'm not going to bloody Buncrana,' complained a civil servant called Gráinne, except she didn't say 'bloody'. 'The Dubs are being left behind again. It's a big issue around here. First it was Ray McSharry and Sligo. Then it was Albert Reynolds and Longford and now it's that silly woman and Buncrana,' she said. 'What about those of us who want to live here in Cabra?'

'You just don't want to leave Paradise,' teased Nicky Kehoe. Mary Lou said Sinn Féin was in favour of decentralisation as long as it was voluntary.

Another man said he worked in a building with 800 public servants and only 38 had applied for decentralisation. 'I was born in this house. I've lived all my life in Cabra. I want to stay here. I'm good at my job, but they're going to take it away. Decentralisation was all very well for people in agriculture and fisheries,' he said. 'Not for Dubs.'

Have you any Europeanny issues, Mary Lou asked voters hopefully, but they didn't. Nicky Kehoe was more to the point. 'Did you see her on the telly? he asked. Nicky knows all about the importance of voter recognition.

So well-spoken, well-dressed, at ease, on she marched in the sunshine towards Sinn Féin's first European Parliamentary seat in the Republic. At one stage in Whitefriars Street area, a canvasser pulled her aside to avoid a drunk on his way to the pub. 'Keep away from him. He likes attacking total strangers on the street,' said the canvasser. 'Oh, just like the Workers' Party, then?' joked one Sinn Féiner, raising echoes of the old and often violent inter-necine battles between the Provisional Republicans and the Official movement which became the Workers' Party. 'Now, now,' admonished Mary Lou. 'None of that.'

The past, you see, is another country and as far as this wench is concerned, it's dead.

Loyal Lieutenants

Two people stand out from the local and European election circus of 2004: John O'Donoghue of Fianna Fáil and Frank Flannery of Fine Gael. And they stand out for one particular reason: loyalty.

After Fianna Fáil's European and local election debacle, when there wasn't a Taoiseach, nor hardly a senior government minister anywhere to be seen, John O'Donoghue, cabinet minister and Fianna Fáil Director of European elections, sat there and took all the brickbats. The first time I saw John speaking on a Fianna Fáil platform in Kerry in the early eighties, he chanted his party speech in that plaintive tenor voice with his eyes closed, a bit like a tortured *sean-nós* singer. He still has that tortured air, that look of wishing he was elsewhere, and he must have wished himself anywhere else over the post-election weekend. He sat there in the RTÉ studio as Fianna Fáil's Brian Crowley aimed an Exocet at him from the count in Cork where Fianna Fáil were losing their second European Munster seat. 'If you had let us roam the constituency, we could have built a vote outside the party support,' complained Crowley, 'but you didn't and now you see the result.'

With open scorn from Crowley, followed by disdain from a beaten Jim McDaid, followed by endless probing from interviewers, O'Donoghue's expression went from troubled, to tortured, to plumb miserable. Short of pouring the contents of a teapot over his head like the dormouse from *Alice in Wonderland*, you wondered if there was any further humiliation they could heap on him. But he took it all, hours and hours of it and muttered repeatedly, like a mantra, the late Labour leader Frank Cluskey's answer as to why Fianna Fáil hadn't won. 'Well, we just didn't get enough votes.' It was desperate. It was admirable. It was loyal.

On the other side of the fence was Frank Flannery, Fine Gael's Director of Local Elections. A brilliant strategist, a man who believes that all the important battles are first won in the backrooms, Flannery has worked voluntarily in those backrooms through three decades and a succession of Fine Gael leaders except for Michael Noonan. When everyone decided after the disaster of the last election that the party was truly over, Flannery continued to hope; to give shape to fellow Mayoman Enda Kenny's leadership; to help plan the extraordinary surge in membership; and to plan the efficient candidate distribution in the local elections. It was he who urged that Fine Gael play all its aces in the European election, fielding a personality-led team ideal for the massive European constituencies, even at the risk of creating great gaps in the party frontbench. When he forecast the party's local and European success, he was laughed at. Well, they're not laughing now.

Loyalty in politics has become a much underrated virtue. In these individualistic times, we give more attention to the maverick, the one who breaks ranks, who complains loudest. But loyalty is central to the whole political process. People like it. There's nothing that puts voters off a party more than disloyalty. Look what happened to Fine Gael when it kept on killing off its leaders. Look what happened to Fianna Fáil with the constant disloyalty inspired by Charlie Haughey. Look what happened to the Tories in Britain. Disloyalty and infighting made them unelectable. Voters reckon that if party colleagues can't trust one another, then we can't trust them either.

Fianna Fáil got its bout of disloyalty over after the election disaster and quickly packed McCreevy off into European exile. With three years and fuller coffers, they should be well able to prepare the ground for a better result in the general election. But still, these results show that Sinn Féin has taken a slice of their vote and may take seats from them in a general election. If Fine Gael continue successfully to pull back support from the PDs, then the PDs won't be sufficient to make up a coalition. At this point, at least, Fine Gael, Labour and the Greens seem to be lining up together so who's on offer to Fianna Fáil? Sinn Féin and the Independents? Suddenly, for those who are queasy about Sinn Féin in government, the notion of a Fine Gael-led alternative takes on a whole new attraction.

And watching an embattled and loyal John O'Donoghue get into close combat with Mary Lou McDonald of Sinn Féin on 'Questions and Answers' after the election, you had a sense of Fianna Fáil meeting its nemesis. You knew O'Donoghue had properly identified the real enemy, but you knew too that close combat could soon become a political embrace. And what happens to those constitutional nationalist parties who embrace Sinn Féin? Look North at the SDLP and you'll know. Just look North.

Black Magic and By-elections

All elections at some stage will bring out the witch doctors with their boxes of black political tricks. But there's something about by-elections that foments a particular voodoo. Politicians get too clever by half during by-elections.

In 1982, in what he thought was a major political stroke, Charlie Haughey appointed Fine Gael's Dick Burke to the EU Commission, causing a by-election in Dublin West. Haughey was confident he would win a much-needed Fianna Fáil seat.

However, John Boland, Fine Gael's Director of Elections and a master of the dark arts, pulled off one of the greatest ever by-election victories when Fine Gael won with Liam Skelly. Flushed with success, Fine Gael set about using the same tactics in the Galway East by-election later that year: saturation canvassing, punishing schedules – and the trick thought to have swung Dublin West: a 6am leaflet drop on Election Day which began cheerily, 'Good morning, voter.'

It was the job of then Fine Gael Senator and UCD Politics Lecturer, Maurice Manning, whose father came from

Woodford, to start delivering leaflets there at the more acceptable rural hour of 7am. When Manning arrived, there wasn't a Fine Gael canvasser or a local to be seen. So he started by himself, walking down a totally deserted street, pushing leaflets through the letterboxes of sleeping houses. Eventually, a woman came to the door to see Maurice delivering what she thought was her post. 'And I thought,' she said pityingly, 'that you had a great job altogether up in Dublin'.

Fine Gael didn't win. What works in Dublin West doesn't work in Galway East. It was Fianna Fáil's Noel Treacy who won, securing the last by-election victory for any Irish government.

That's why governments hate by-elections. For governments, by-elections are expensive and difficult. Every local lobby group uses the opportunity to demand concessions. Canvassing, particularly in the winter, is notoriously hard on ministers and deputies who come down with colds and flu and miss vital votes as well as departmental duties. One deputy bought herself a specially warm leather coat for standing in the wind tunnels outside shopping centres in Meath and Kildare.

But Oppositions love by-elections, because immediately they're put on a more equal media footing with the government – the media has to give them equal coverage. Oppositions have more time to spend canvassing. They can make mischief.

If there's dissent in the Opposition party, however, by-elections can be dangerous. In the South Tipperary by-election of 2000, it was noticed that a number of John Bruton's opponents in Fine Gael would arrive in the area, spend some time swanning around the local hotel and then leave without canvassing a vote. As it happens, Fine Gael's Tom Hayes did very well against the surge of votes which elected Independent Séamus Healy. But it's still felt that a little more concerted Fine Gael effort might have won Fine Gael the seat – as it did in the by-election of 2001.

Questions equally were asked about Fianna Fáil's poor performance and it's notable that local deputy Noel Davern is no longer a Junior Minister and has announced he will retire.

But then, by-elections are a nightmare for the sitting TD. The incumbent is setting up a rival. Often they get their retaliation in first and try to ensure that a no-hoper is nominated. That's fine as long as they are happy to stay on the backbenches.

Then there are by-election strokes. Most famous is Ray Burke's planting of trees at a Dublin West housing estate, which were ripped out again the day after Fianna Fáil lost the seat. Schools and hospitals which have already been launched and opened are launched and opened again to great fanfare. In South Tipperary, when local unemployment was a major issue, Mary Harney came down to open a shed in Clonmel. It was trumpeted as an advance factory, but journalists were astonished to find themselves in what they assumed was a hay barn. In Cork in 1994, before the smoking ban, Kathleen Lynch would plead breathing problems before any of the long radio panel discussions. After forty smoke-free minutes, her cigarette-addicted opponents would be reduced to pulp.

And, of course, the pressure is greatest on the candidates themselves. Often, they are running for the seat of a dead husband or father or mother or brother and there are memories and grief all along the way. There's usually a pact among the other parties that they don't publicly attack the candidate whose party had held the seat. There's a feeling that you respect the territory once held by another party, that you tread carefully or you will lose transfers.

And then, if by election candidates get elected, they're made for political life. They almost always get re-elected, getting credit, no matter what their party, for the extra facilities that local pressure groups always manage to extract from the government during by-elections. The pressure and exposure isn't so welcome for families, though. In South Tipperary, Tom Hayes' family had to go through it all twice.

At one stage, his party, Fine Gael, wanted to make a point about youth facilities. They needed a picture of

Tom with some youngsters and they needed it fast. So he had to recruit his own mutinous teenagers. 'Would you believe, in the end,' says Tom, 'I had to pay them'

Now there's a pair of youngsters who understand what by-elections are all about.

NORTHERN LIGHTS

A Tale of Two Cities

It was thirty years ago in Belfast and my unionist colleague felt I didn't really appreciate the place. 'After all,
this is the city,' he boasted, 'which built the *Titanic*.'
When I pointed out mildly that the *Titanic* sank – and on
its first voyage – he hit the roof. 'Typical Southerner!' he
raged. 'You understand nothing about Northern Ireland
and you never will.'

But in time I came to love Belfast. I came to understand how it yearned for its great industrial past, and just
how symbolic those giant gantries on the skyline really
were. I was sad moving back to Dublin, and as I sat
squeezed in between them in the front of their van, the
two removal men, one from the Shankill, the other from
Newtownards, quizzed me. 'What's a nice wee girl like
you doing moving back to a Popish state where the
priests rule your bedroom?' they asked. They were horri-
fied at getting stuck in Dublin overnight, and at the sug-
gestion that they might go to a B and B. 'We'll sleep in
the van,' they said piously.

I missed Belfast. I missed the fierceness of its loves and
hates, the vitality of the daily debate, the black, black

sense of humour. Dublin seemed effete, somehow, and shallow. Because we're very different, North and South. Conor Cruise O'Brien put it well when he said that Northerners are like dogs – in your face and barking. Southerners are like cats – we purr, but we have hidden claws.

I was thinking about those differences when I looked back at 'Through Irish Eyes', the survey of Irish attitudes towards the UK published by the British Council and the British Embassy. Because in that survey, Northern Ireland was the dog that didn't bark. In the Republic, we were all congratulating ourselves on the evidence of improved relations with the UK, but when we looked at the one part of that United Kingdom which is on our own island, the news wasn't so good. Many of us felt much more positive about Scotland and Wales than we did about Northern Ireland. Only half of us had visited Northern Ireland, whereas 84% had visited London. That survey was taken among third-level-educated under-40s. It's worse when you go to the wider population, as Co-operation Ireland did in 2001. That survey found that only 41% have ever been North.

There are lots of reasons why we're more likely to go to Britain than to Northern Ireland. As well as being put off by the Troubles, there's the whole pattern of emigration. We have more family links in London and Manchester and are more likely to have lived there than in Northern Ireland.

But what about other links which you would expect to

exist but which don't? Take trade. You might expect that we would trade well with the other part of our island, particularly since the Peace Process. But no, we conduct little merchandise trade. In 2002, only 1.8% of Ireland's total merchandise export earnings came from export sales to Northern Ireland. Only 1.9% of Ireland's total merchandise import bill was accounted for by goods from Northern Ireland. In fact, for the first half of 2003, the value of our merchandise exports to Switzerland was twice as high as to Northern Ireland.

And these figures have social as well as economic implications. They are lost opportunities for human contact, for interdependence, for joint development. Because where things are done jointly, the links exist. Take sport. We do showjumping and rugby on a thirty-two county basis. And those friendships hold. Trevor Ringland, member of the UUP and a legendary Irish rugby hero, is a familiar face on sporting and charitable committees South and North as is his colleague, Dubliner Hugo McNeill. Those links help us to understand and confront differences.

We could try harder. In the 'Through Irish Eyes' survey, 50% of us said we wanted to take part in North/South reconciliation projects, but only 4% of us actually did. And this is despite all the good work done by Co-operation Ireland; by the Ireland Funds; by the International Fund for Ireland; through joint operations by the two employers' bodies, IBEC and the CBI; and by the trades unions. Our eyes still glaze over when there's an item about the North on television. We still skip over the Northern news pages in the paper.

That's partly because we are so very different. In the Republic, we now have a modernised economy with an expanded private sector. Northern Ireland is still adapting from another industrial era and is heavily subsidised from London. The differences are there in the tale of two cities: Belfast is Victorian, solid industrial redbrick; Dublin is flighty Georgian. Belfast's settled working class stayed for generations in the same areas, inheriting jobs and houses, and daughters lived around the corner from their mothers. Dublin's population was always mobile, moving out, moving on. In Dublin, a street may be more likely to be made up of blow-ins like me from the country, rather than 'real Dubs'.

Northerners are different in other ways. I pointed out to one Belfast friend the endless ads for sofas on Ulster television. '*Why* do Northerners buy so many sofas?' I asked him. 'Because they want to stay at home in comfort with their families,' he answered sternly, 'instead of gadding about all the time like you lot. You're flighty. On Good Friday, or Stephen's Day, when everything's closed, you're still out prowling, looking for any dogfight where you might find a crowd and a drink. Why don't you just stay at home?'

Northerners aren't like us and they're not terribly interested in us. Indeed, many of them have a fairly vague handle on the Republic. I know a Dubliner who recently bought … yes a sofa from a place on Boucher Road in Belfast. He went to check on details for delivery to find it was all efficiently wrapped and ready to be despatched. But when he went to make sure it had the right Dublin address, he discovered that all it bore was the immortal designation: 'Down South'.

Dropping your 'H's

Northern commentator Fionnuala O'Connor sees what others miss. That's partly because she keeps watch after the cameras and lights have moved on. It happened once when she was reporting for *The Irish Times* at the 1984 Ulster Unionist conference. The official message from the conference was one of moderation, no triumphalism towards nationalist opponents. But after the big names had moved off stage to take a break, Fionnuala stayed on to listen to a badly attended lunchtime debate on Ulster Culture. A delegate attacked the new voices he was hearing on BBC Radio Ulster. 'How often I have been irritated, as I'm sure you must have been, by that dreadful pronunciation "haitch",' he said. There was laughter, and as Fionnuala O'Connor explained: 'For those unaccustomed to the fine points of Northern anthropology: the pronunciation of an aspirate "haitch" is deemed to denote Catholicism, much as shifty eyes do, or coal in the bath.'

Her report of the delegate's speech continued: 'Where did it come from? I hate the "haitch", beamed Councillor Ward, buoyant on a sea of chuckles, the best audience of his life. 'Give me the native Ulster "aitch".'

And then Councillor Ward came to the point, listing some of the names which he said had 'crept' into the BBC. Among them were Terry Wogan and Frank Delaney. All of them, in origin at least, were identifiably Catholic.

The fact that his audience enjoyed it so much was depressing, because this wasn't the DUP. It was the supposedly moderate Official Unionist Party and it wasn't that long ago. But perhaps the reason the phonetics lesson took centre stage then was that this was the letter which had dominated Irish politics for the previous three years: 'haitch' as in H-Blocks – or, if you prefer, 'aitch'-blocks.

The H-Blocks protest at the Maze Prison outside Belfast, where republican prisoners went on hunger-strike to achieve political status, was a shadow which hung over North and South in the long hot summer of 1981. With Bobby Sands dead and nine others to die, the country was draped in black flags. They were all over Donegal where I was on holiday; ranged all up the avenue to Countess Markievicz's home at Lissadell and at Yeats' grave at Drumcliff in Sligo. Overnight they appeared on Harold's Cross Bridge, near where I lived in Dublin.

In Cairo in October, covering the funeral of assassinated President Anwar Sadat, I called into an Egyptian newspaper to find what they were saying next day. The bescarfed, young woman night editor, who came to help me, spoke little English. I told her I was from Ireland. Her face lit up. 'Ah, Bobby Sands,' she breathed reverently. After all, Islam, like Catholicism, knew all about martyrs.

And, of course, that's what the hunger strike did. It gave the Republican movement contemporary martyrs, martyrs who died by their own hand. It also gave them the drug to which they have now become addicted, electoral politics. Nationalists who would never have supported the IRA rowed in behind the hunger-strikers. It was when Gerry Adams saw the massive vote for Bobby Sands and Owen Carron in the two Fermanagh-South Tyrone elections, and the election of two hunger-strike TDs to Dáil Éireann, that he saw the potential electoral support available to Sinn Féin on a non-violent issue.

Still, even with the twenty-fifth anniversary and the important place they hold in Republican liturgy, I was surprised that such a central position was given to the hunger-strikers at the 2006 Sinn Féin Ard-Fheis. This, after all, is new post-IRA Sinn Féin, trendy, electable, forward-looking, with a platform of shiny hip young women delegates who looked as though they'd wandered off the screens of TG4. They were obviously meant to represent the future face of Sinn Féin and they were in stark contrast to the emphasis on past icons: the hunger-strikers' photographs around the restaurant; the build-up on live television to the leader's speech which ignored Adams and consisted instead of an emotional tribute to Bobby Sands by Michelle Gildernew. Then there was

Adams' own constant reference to the hunger strikers, layering Bobby Sands and the older generation of 1916 martyrs in and out throughout his speech like mothballs.

But then you came to realise that preservation was exactly what Adams was at. It's when a movement is stretching furthest from its roots, perilously so, that it needs to hold tightest to traditional icons.

After all, here is a leadership which has in the last year brought about the announcement of a final decommissioning. Here is a leadership which had a difficult weekend and had to step in sharpish to ensure the door was left open to supporting the Northern Ireland Policing board and the PSNI; and to ensure that no blanket ban was put on Sinn Féin joining a future coalition government. Ending the war; keeping open the possibility of backing the police; leaving doors open to coalition government – that's a long stretch from irredentist, abstentionist, militant Republicanism. You have to find a way to bring the troops with you.

There was a time when all moves away from the war were validated by the reassuring presence on the platform of veteran IRA man Joe Cahill. But Joe's dead. Time now to wrap yourself in the martyr's flag, the Che Guevara image of Bobby Sands, and the blood sacrifice of 1916.

But then, I suppose, they're doing what almost every other party does: Fianna Fáil with Pearse; Fine Gael with Collins; Labour with Connolly. I've never been a great one for digging up the dead myself. However, if that's what it takes to complete the move to constitutional politics, so be it, I suppose.

Better to be celebrating the old martyrs than planning to create new ones.

THE LIVING
AND THE DEAD

Lest We Forget

In the world of television, there's a place where all the real action happens. No, not the studio. It's the hospitality room, or in TV slang, the hostility room. Here, before or usually after a programme, the guests feel free to say what they really think, and usually it's far more interesting than what they say on air.

After one television discussion, the then minister in the Haughey cabinet, Martin O'Donoghue, and Fine Gael frontbencher, John Kelly, were having a well-earned drink and a heated discussion. Though they were political opponents, they liked one another. They were both university professors – Martin Professor of Economics in Trinity, John Professor of Law in UCD. They were both passionate about classical music and knowing O'Donoghue to be like himself – civilised, educated, upright – John Kelly proceeded to remonstrate with Martin about being part of Haughey's cabinet and therefore associated with Haughey's opportunism and his brand of green nationalism.

Never a man to understate his case, Kelly waded in deep. 'How can you, Martin,' he expostulated, 'sit in that dank cave where moral turpitude drips from the stalactites and the bats fly from side to side?' Martin, usually a mild man, bristled. He took it to be an attack on Fianna Fáil and he let fly. He might be a professor but he had waited tables in Jammet's Restaurant to pay for his education, he said furiously – he hadn't come from a comfortable background like Kelly. And that's why he was in Fianna Fáil, because it included everybody. And Fianna Fáil, he said, also took as its historic responsibility the need to include those of strong republican views, to shepherd them past the temptation to turn to guns, to give them a constitutional political home. Fianna Fáil could have sat in its ivory tower and played holier-than-thou like Fine Gael, raged Martin, but it took its historic responsibilities seriously. And that was why it was electorally the size it was, he concluded with a flourish, and that was why Fine Gael was the size it was.

Well, this was as good a discussion of the difference between Irish political parties as I had ever heard and I only wished I had managed to prompt it live on air. And I remember watching Fianna Fáil leaders continue that historic task of trying to bring Republicans in from the militaristic cold and finally, it seemed, succeeding. By the time the Good Friday Agreement was signed and confirmed in 1998, you began to wonder if the time had come when Northern Ireland would no longer be the dividing line in Irish politics, when we could stop rowing over who were the true descendants of the nationalist martyrs, when we could stop, as the Paul Brady song says, 'trying to carve tomorrow from a tombstone.' I remember thinking that maybe at Easter, in future, we might commemorate the Good Friday Agreement's brave new start for all of us instead of concentrating, as we have always done, on digging up the dead.

But no. Having helped bring Provisional Republicans at least halfway in from the political cold, Fianna Fáil has also created a political rival. With elections looming, a new round of scuffling has broken out over who the real Republicans are.

It's been like this for as long as I can remember, particularly around Easter. The parties tramp from graveyard to graveyard exhuming the Fenian dead: Fianna Fáil in Arbour Hill; Sinn Féin in Glasnevin. And in an attempt at republican swagger, we had a disappointing return to the old Civil War hostilities at Kilcrumper Cemetery in Fermoy, County Cork. The then Finance Minister Charlie McCreevy said that the real founders of the Irish State were the men and women of 1916 and not those who took power in 1922. Well, now maybe Charlie, they both had a hand in it and it's depressing to think you're back to this old guff again. Mind you, Fine Gael gets down to its own annual piece of necrophilia in the summer when they commemorate Michael Collins at Béal na Bláth. And then, never one to be left out, we have Justice Minister, Michael McDowell, trying to make sure Sinn Féin and the IRA aren't allowed any claim over the Republicanism of

1916 to 1923 and they're all at it again, fighting over the bodies, fighting over the past.

If we really want to honour those who died for this country, you know, a little silence mightn't go amiss. It's always struck me that silence may show more respect than this endless knocking on the coffins of the patriot dead, begging for posthumous recognition.

And there's a place to do it. The British do it at the Cenotaph. We could stand in Kilmainham Jail, and let the cold of those stones seep into our bones, and remember how it must have been for Connolly and Clarke and Pearse and their comrades as they waited to be hauled out into that yard to be shot. Maybe that's what we should do, to think of them not as historic icons but as the real people they were, brave and foolhardy and still hopeful; to stand in that historic place and remember them with our silence, and then to let them rest in peace.

Something to Celebrate

Everybody has their own slice of 1916. For us, as children, it was the autograph book and the piano. The autograph book had pale pink and green and yellow pages – and it was full of verses, of jokes, of little sketches, the same sort of stuff as schoolgirls put in except that these were prisoners in Knutsford and Reading jails, all transported there after the Easter Rising. Among them were Liam Mellows, Cathal O'Shannon, Seán T O'Kelly, Terence McSwiney, Darrell Figgis, Ernest Blythe, Tomás MacCurtain and Seán Milroy, all of whom signed their names in Irish including my own grandfather whose book it was, Eamonn Dundon. The sketch by Seán Milroy was of a cell in the jail. The verses were typically Edwardian – a mixture of sentiment and religious piety and heroism – and the jokes were Edwardian too, sort of innocent.

His book was kept in a battered leather case with his jail mug and towel and it was these simple humdrum things that my mother showed us, not his handgun, nor the rifles found under the floorboards in our linenpress, not his medals or the whole bloody warmongery of the time. She was proud of him but she didn't believe in glorifying violence. So it was only many years later I discovered he'd been officer in command of the Fourth Battalion, Carlow Brigade, IRA, or as they referred to themselves then, the Volunteers. He bought arms on behalf of GHQ early in 1916, stored them at our house in Borris and handed them over to the Kilkenny Volunteers on Easter Monday 1916. It was the receipts for these found in his house afterwards by the RIC, he said, which nearly doomed him to penal servitude for life. He also brought gelignite from Scotland to make the grenades and bombs used in the GPO in 1916.

Carlow wasn't directly involved in fighting in Easter Week though, according to him, they carried arms.

But knowing he was a marked man, he asked the girl he was going out with if she'd marry him. They got married one afternoon at the end of Easter Week in a quiet ceremony in Borris Church, using a wedding ring borrowed from her mother's housekeeper who was also their witness. They walked to Palace East, the nearest train station where he guessed there wouldn't be soldiers. They headed for Kerry, where they were optimistic enough to think they might have a honeymoon. Instead of that, he had to go on the run but was soon arrested and sent eventually to jail in Knutsford and Reading. In this time he shared a cell with IRB head, Dennis McCullough, and used to talk to him about his new wife, how lovely she was, how musical she was, and how he'd never been able to give her a honeymoon or buy her a proper engagement ring or present. 'Buy her a piano,' said McCullough who ran a piano business in Belfast, as he was later to do in Dublin. So my grandfather did and the Schiedmayer was ordered from jail. I still have it.

So we knew about the piano and about the autograph book. We knew almost nothing about the gelignite and the rifles and the fighting and long periods in and out of jail right up to the end of the War of Independence. My grandfather wouldn't talk about it to his own children and we knew my grandmother never wholly approved of it.

As the Northern troubles got worse all throughout the seventies and eighties, my mother wouldn't talk about it at all. There was a feeling that these things were better forgotten, better buried and forgotten than dug up in a way that might be used to justify bloodshed.

It could be said that the state felt much the same, that it was better to play down the enabling myth, to cancel the annual military celebration of 1916. And it's because most republican violence, hopefully, has stopped, that we were able to celebrate the ninetieth anniversary as we did the fiftieth with great fanfare, if less republican triumphalism. But there's something else common to 1966 and now: prosperity, and a sense of self-confidence. In the sixties, we had an economic foretaste of what's happened now. We were starting to sustain our own citizens as we do now. Then came the devastation of the fifties, when whole townslands out around the hills of Mount Leinster left for Birmingham and Manchester. Six per cent of the population of this country emigrated in the terrible eighties and the farewell scenes at air and sea ports after Christmas would break your heart. I remember people telling me that they were going to follow their children who had had to leave for Australia or the US or the UK. 'How can I call this my country,' said one woman, 'when my own children can't live here?' It was hard to be proud of a country which couldn't keep its people. Emigration did as much to corrode the soul of Irish nationalism as did republican violence.

Now we can all live here. And our children can live here. Not as equally as we would like, nor cherished in the way the Proclamation envisaged. But they're here and lots more with them. The population is expanding. And that also gives a country a sense of self-worth.

Indeed, it could be said that the last ten years of boom have finally validated this state.

Rightly or wrongly we see history through today's eyes. So when the magnificent army band leads off the 1916 ceremonies in Dublin city centre, I won't actually be celebrating gelignite or rifles, or even so much the courage of the men who were brought out to be shot at dawn ninety years ago. I'll be celebrating the fact that finally and for the foreseeable future, my child can live here. And so can yours.

Up the Republic!

Remembering Dan

Watching the ceremony celebrating the 90th anniversary of the Easter Rising in the main street of our capital city, I was delighted to see that no full shot of the event could avoid the great statue of Daniel O'Connell. O'Connell is my great hero in Irish history. It was right that on a happier and more positive day of celebration than almost any other I can remember, Dan should be present whether formally acknowledged or not.

Yes, his peaceful methods were at odds with those of 1916, but they wanted the same thing: an end to the union. However, it always seemed to me that Dan stood for something bigger, stretching well beyond Ireland or the constraints of his own time. As Fintan O'Toole has pointed out, he was the father not only of Irish democracy but also of mass democracy. He became my hero, because even as a child I understood that he included me. At primary school, all the stars of history were warriors – from Brian Boru to Art MacMurrough Kavanagh, to O'Neill and O'Donnell, to Wolfe Tone and Pearse. War wasn't what girls did, certainly not in the fifties, so Irish history to me was like football. Traditionally your only role as a woman was to make the sandwiches. I never liked making the sandwiches.

But Dan let me on the pitch, because he was about words and I loved words. I can still remember sitting in the brown desks at primary school and being told how he could hold an audience in the palm of his hand; how he once took on a foul-mouthed fishwife and how he silenced her with a string of exotic insults without ever once using a foul word. But most of all I remember how in 1843, the year of the monster meetings supporting the Repeal of the Act of Union between Ireland and Great Britain, he called off the great meeting in Clontarf when it was banned by the authorities. He would not take the risk that the thousands who would come to listen to his words would be exposed to bloodshed. As a nine-year-old, I remember thinking how eminently sensible this was. And I could never understand why eminently sensible adults like my teachers hinted that Dan had somehow bottled out, and that the bloody suppression of the massive Clontarf meeting was exactly what the country then needed.

As I grew up, I came to understand how modern he was, and how, as an individualist, he accepted the principle of full equality for women. 'Mind,' he said once, 'has no sex.' He was a liberal in every sense. He was a leading figure in the European campaign to abolish slavery. He supported religious freedom for all, dissenters as well as Catholics. He was an economic liberal and would have felt perfectly at home with Ireland's open, globalised economy. After all, he was opposed to trade barriers and supported the repeal of the corn laws. He was a champion of low taxes. An entrepreneur himself, he helped to found the precursors of the National Bank and the Alliance and Dublin Gas Company.

And as someone who's observed parliament in Dublin and London, I came to appreciate what a star he had been in Westminster. One English parliamentary observer in 1837, no political supporter of O'Connell's, describes his dark green coat and his brown wig and goes on: 'He always wears his hat cocked on the right side of his head, in the manner so common among sailors. His whole appearance, indeed, is like that of a ship's captain for which he is often taken by strangers.' And then he describes his speaking powers: 'Mr. O'Connell is a man of the highest order of genius. There is not a member of the house who, in this respect, can for a moment be put in comparison with him. You see the greatness of his genius in almost every sentence he utters. ... It ever and anon bursts forth with a brilliancy and effect which are quite overwhelming ... you are taken captive wherever the speaker chooses to lead you, from beginning to end.'

When Ireland needed his eloquence most, O'Connell was dying. The historian WEH Lecky quotes Disraeli's picture of him as he appeared for the last time in the House of Commons in 1847 to plead for Famine Aid: 'an old, feeble, broken-hearted man, murmuring amid the deep silence of the House the few pathetic words which were only audible to those who were near him: "Ireland is in your hands ... I solemnly call on you to recollect that I predict with the sincerest conviction that a quarter of her population will perish unless you come to her relief."' Three months later Daniel O'Connell himself was dead.

We can be proud of everything he did, everything he was: liberal, democrat, fervent Irish man and Kerryman, in tune with our times and the peace we have now. If Easter is to be our chosen time of national celebration then O'Connell must be part of it. Still, I was glad to see how his monument dominated events anyway in the street we called after him. Because as long as Dan is there, we're all included.

Living

I grew up in *Wind-in-the-Willows* country – a place of dazzling weirs, and grassy banks and otters swimming beside you in the silky water. That's how I saw it. That's how I still see it. But there was a dark side, too. Every so often, usually in the winter, we'd hear of people who had thrown themselves into the river in flood, or into the deep waters of the canal locks. When I'd ask my mother why, she'd just shake her head wordlessly.

Nobody wanted to talk about it, but we all felt diminished. I suppose central to our primal sense of self-preservation is a sense of life's joy, of its endless possibilities. And suicide dealt a blow to that. If those people didn't feel life was worth living, were they right, we began to ask?

But, of course, we didn't ask out loud. We didn't talk about it. There were the families to consider and to add to their terrible grief was the fact that suicide was still a crime. France decriminalised it in 1892; Britain in 1967, but in that year Ireland was still pursuing through the courts people who had attempted suicide.

It remained a crime up until 1993. And, of course, it

was regarded as a sin of despair – Judas Iscariot's sin. The Roman Catholic Church wouldn't bury people who'd committed suicide in consecrated ground, or give them a funeral Mass.

That's changed. What hasn't changed is that we still don't talk about it. And it's vital that we do because it's got worse, particularly among young men. If you strip out the new accession states, we have the worst rate of suicide among young men in the EU. And that has increased almost fourfold in twenty years. Many reasons are put forward: drug and alcohol abuse; sexual abuse; loneliness and bullying; marital or job problems. But whatever the initial cause, the big common factor in suicide is a significant psychiatric disorder, very often depression. As three professors of psychiatry pointed out at a conference run by the 3Ts (Turning the Tide) campaign group, it's as plain as the nose on your face that we need to improve mental health services.

So why don't we shout about it as we do about cancer treatment and hip operations? Why don't we shout about the fact that a smaller and smaller proportion of the health budget is going to mental health? The Inspectorate of Mental Health said in 2004 that 'compared with ten years earlier, the share of funding spend on mental health had halved.' If someone in your family feels suicidal tomorrow, there's no national suicide crisis centre with a twenty-four-hour, seven-day helpline and expertise. We closed down most of the big mental hospitals in the sixties and the seventies, but we didn't transfer the resources as promised into community care. There are very few community-based state services, where psychiatric, psychological and psychotherapeutic help is readily available. Only 50% of GPs or A and E doctors have had post-graduate psychiatric training. There are private psychiatric facilities in affluent areas like Dublin's Southside but very little in poorer areas. It's often voluntary organisations like the Samaritans, or bereavement groups set up to help families of those who've committed suicide, who are getting the calls for help.

But we don't protest and march up and down in front of the Dáil with banners, because of the stigma still attached in this country to mental illness, the feeling that it shames the family. And because we stay silent, we lose people. Because we stay silent, we let politicians off the hook. I've suffered from depression, but somebody spotted it in time and got me help. Other people may not be so lucky and because they can't speak for themselves when they're depressed or despairing, the rest of us have to do their shouting for them.

We have to challenge them with the fact that they're not alone, that they do belong to something bigger than themselves; that with treatment and help, they will once again feel that life, for all its faults, is worth living. Because we have a common interest here. The older I get, the more I am drawn to people who hunger for life. Chancers and scoundrels though some of them may be, their joie de vivre warms me too, adds to the common life force which sustains us all. Everyone we lose to suicide diminishes that force, diminishes each one of us. We all have our place, as the American poet Mary Oliver puts it, 'in the family of things'.

An Imperfect Education

It was a Saturday night in 1967. We were wandering home from the Literary and Historical Society in UCD, me and a bookish type who was explaining about poetry and metre and the three-syllable dactyl and the two-syllable trochee. Down the stairs from Kirwan House pub tumbled a drunken student. As he hit the pavement, he howled plaintively into the wastes of Leeson Street: 'Hanrahan, you hungry hooer, come back with me coat.' My bookish companion didn't miss a beat. 'There you are, you see: a perfect dactyl, "hanrahan",' he explained crisply, 'and the two-syllable trochees: "hungry" and the vernacular "hooer".'

I was struck at that moment by two great truths: first, that this was high-class stuff my learned friend was spouting; second, that on the whole I'd rather be drinking with Hanrahan and the hungry whores. And there you have the story of my less-than-brilliant career at university.

That was the good part. The bad part was a college that was, as Ruairí Quinn has termed it, not so much a university as 'a Catholic Boys' Academy'. Almost all the professors in my area, the Arts faculty, were male and many of them were priests. The front row seats of every lecture theatre were bagged by lines of nuns and seminarians. Girls were forbidden to wear trousers. There was no doubt that this was a Catholic University and that His Grace the Archbishop ruled here.

The place was an educational slum. Lecture halls were overcrowded, the tutorial system was hit and miss. There was no student representation on the governing body. When we all heard in 1968/69 that we would be moved to the Belfield campus, where a wonderful new church was in place but no proper library facilities, no student residences, well, we were ripe for revolution.

And we had it, the gentle revolution in 68/69, a wonderful time of marches and sit-ins and Alan Stivell concerts. Sr Ben, the historian Margaret McCurtain, was one of the select band of lecturers who could be certain of her welcome with a student audience. She pleaded with us in the Great Hall for a little understanding of the bewildered old men whose university had come to a standstill. I still remember the feeling of power that gave us, and I know I learned more about power and politics in those few months than ever before or since.

To have that time and that space was a great, great privilege. Years later, I was chatting to Nuala O'Faolain about how awful UCD was in its John Charles McQuaid days, when Mary Kenny butted in. 'I've been sitting here listening to you two whinging about your time at university,' she raged. 'How dare you! Have you ever thought what it was like for the rest of us, stuck in secretarial colleges and dead-end jobs? You were so very lucky.'

We were. There were only 16,000 of us in third level then, as compared with 120,000 now, and university gave us career choices, confidence, earning power ... as it does for today's graduates. And there's the nub.

We're told there's a funding crisis in universities. Danny O'Hare, former head of Dublin City University, says the sector needs 200 million euros a year more.

Fair enough. Is it fair, however, that the state, which already provides 85% of university funding, should have to come up with 200 million more?

How can any government justify such a massive provision from the education budget when there are still children leaving primary school who can't read or write; and when there is no system of national pre-school education which would go some way towards addressing the education effects of social disadvantage?

Yes, the universities need funds. It's disturbing to hear of cut-backs in teaching staff, teaching hours, library access. The teaching of undergraduates remains, to my mind, the primary role of a university – research is important, but secondary. New funds should be ploughed mainly into teaching.

The extra funds, however, should be provided, in some part, by those who benefit economically and socially from a university education. I couldn't have afforded to go to college if Carlow County Council hadn't paid for me, for which I'm eternally grateful. But can I now afford to pay for my child's university fees? Yes, like so much of middle-class Dublin, I can. State aid should be targeted instead on providing generous fee and maintenance grants for students from families with low incomes.

Almost every major report on third-level education has argued that university fees should be restored. It's ironic that though free fees were introduced by the Irish Labour Party, it's the PDs who recognise what a subsidy they are to the middle class and who now most rigorously defend them. Indeed the Tories in the UK recognised them as a potential vote-winner with their supporters in the 2005 British election.

So let the privileged undergraduates pay – either through fees, or through working a number of years for the society that educated them, as doctors in the UK are expected to do. And what of those whose education has made them multi-millionaires in the last decade of Irish boom? Any university worth its salt should be able to tap that resource.

We've done well, those of us who've come through third level. It's a scandal that the state carries our kids free through university while other kids give up at the age of fifteen because under-funded schools have failed them. We in the middle classes are the hungry whores of the education system. It's about time we paid something back.

The Best Band

It was like a scene from 'Dr Zhivago'. The Phoenix Park was white and glistening. Lines of soldiers stood to attention as the snow gathered on their heads and their shoulders and on the red carpet laid out in front of Áras an Uachtarán for the visiting Hungarian President. Dressed in their splendid new parade hats and greatcoats, the Army No. 1 Band stood impassively for an hour in the freezing cold. Then on cue, without as much as flexing a frozen finger, they swung into the Hungarian national anthem, all played to the exact beat of a full twenty-one-gun salute.

It was as perfect a piece of theatre as I've seen in a long time. As the smoke from the cannons drifted away, everyone pushed inside the Áras for hot tea and buns. But not me. I followed the band because that's what I've done since we were kids marching up and down our hallway with a mouth organ, a plastic trumpet and me bringing up the rear with a wooden spoon and a saucepan slung on string around my neck, all of us murdering Souza's 'Stars and Stripes Forever'.

And the Army No. 1 Band has lots of groupies like me.

Take Bray Head, so-called because he was from … eh … Bray. No matter what the weather, he wore a big Crombie coat and carried an umbrella. Whether they played in Blackrock, or St Stephen's Green, or the Phoenix Park, there he'd be, sitting in the rain in the middle of a desert of empty seats. He always wanted them to play Ponchielli's 'Dance of the Hours' and no matter how often they played it, he'd always want them to play it again.

Bands attract people: fellas dancing along in front, conducting; kids marching alongside playing imaginary cornets; aul wans like me skipping along behind as though to the Pied Piper. Because live music, music in the open air, is magic. Suddenly you have ceremony, you have theatre, you have carnival. And this band makes it so, whether it's on state occasions like the presidential inauguration; or great sporting days like a sunny Aga Khan Cup or a rainy soccer international at Lansdowne Road; or when they play school concerts or park concerts around the country.

The Army No. 1 Band has the range of an orchestra – apart from strings. Forty-five at full strength, they can play anything from Wagner overtures and big operatic selections to pop music. But they do best what they were set up to do, to play military music from the Irish tradition.

When the State was founded, General Richard Mulcahy and his adviser, Dr JF Larchet, brought in the help of leading German bandmaster, Wilhelm Fritz Brase.

The Irish affectionately dubbed him Colonel Fitzbrassy and it was he, with his assistant, Col. Christian Sauerzweig, who started a proper band and arranged Irish tunes for it like 'Kelly, the Boy from Killane', and 'The Harp that once through Tara's Halls'. These joined existing marches like 'St Patrick's Day' and 'Garryowen', the marching tunes of British Army regiments – the Irish Guards or the old RIR based in Clonmel. New arrangements continue to this day, with particularly lovely slow marches like *'Sí Beag, Sí Mór'* and *'Thugamar Féin an Samhradh Linn'*, arranged by the present Defence Forces School of Music Director, Lt Col. Brendan Power.

To join the band is to choose a full-time career in music. They're not like the pipers and buglers attached to each battalion. The band have to keep fit and to know their parade drill, but they don't fight. Most recruits these days have a full third-level degree in music. Some like brother and sister Corporal Áine Doyle, clarinet, and Corporal Lorcan Daly, French horn, played in the National Youth Orchestra. Others like Corporal Patrick Gregan, euphonium, and Sgt Colin Lang, trombone, came in at fourteen and sixteen, when the School of Music did all the training. They auditioned by singing a song – to show they could hold a tune.

Like all musicians, they have a healthy disrespect for one another. When one told me he couldn't play the trombone when he started off, they all shouted, 'And he still can't.' When I asked Sgt Fergus Conaghan what he played besides the oboe, they all shouted: 'Sex symbol, he's a sex symbol.' It turns out, as he explained to me later, that he plays the cymbals when the band parades, because the oboe has a double reed which could choke him if he stumbled into a pothole.

They bring great fun to school concerts and in St Paul's Primary School in North Brunswick Street, Paddy Crosbie's original 'School around the Corner', conductor Commandant Mark Armstrong introduced the kids to all the instruments. To show how brass worked, he got the brass section to play only with their mouthpieces, sounding like ducks as they toot-tooted through the 'Blue Danube'. He let the children do the percussion. He gave them the conductor's baton and hat and let them conduct. They had a ball.

This is a brilliant band, symphonic, versatile, full-throated. They're in demand all over the world but there's one day of the year when they know they will definitely be in Ireland. In March, they will lead off, as they always do, the national celebrations – the St Patrick's Parade in Dublin. And all sorts of floats and tumblers and acrobats will be strutting their stuff, too. But groupies like me, and maybe you, and maybe even Bray Head, well, we'll do what we like best.

We'll just follow the band.

A Weekend in Dublin

It was in Derry that they first perfected the art of Saturday afternoon rioting. Myself and a small boy with red hair got caught once in the seventies as the focus of the riot moved up and down William Street. The two of us ducked into a doorway to shelter from the stones and petrol bombs. As a line of soldiers in riot gear lined up beside us, the violence got worse and I was worried the child would be frightened. Then we heard a scream as a soldier was hit on the shoulder. As the squaddie doubled up in pain, the lovely little boy ran over to him. 'Pity it wasn't your friggin' head,' said the kid and ran off.

Those were more savage times, and I suppose we hoped they were over. So coming home from Heuston Station one weekend, I walked quite happily up to O'Connell Bridge to see the Love Ulster march. I used to go up to Belfast in the seventies to see the 12 July march. Now here were unionists and Northern bands, who, instead of shouting across the border, chose to make their protest here. At least they were connecting with Dublin. This, I thought, was a piece of history.

Except that it was a piece of the same old history. Even

the smell of burning petrol as you turned into O'Connell Street brought you back twenty-five, thirty-five years. I remember my uncle Ned warning me as we stood at meetings outside the Guild Hall in Derry: 'Look out for fellas with their hands behind their backs.' Sure enough as I walked up O'Connell Street, a young man in denims came along with his hands behind his back. As he passed, I saw the lump of builders' rubble in his fist. Then he broke into a long loping run and lobbed it over the front-line rioters at the phalanx of Garda shields half way up O'Connell Street. The rocks started to fly. 'I'd get off the street, Missus, if I was you,' said a young man in a Republic of Ireland scarf. And then he shouted at all the youngsters perched on the O'Connell and Larkin monument to stop hanging back taking photographs. 'Get up to the front and do something,' he said. The youngsters stayed put watching. One girl wore a white t-shirt which said: 'The only weapon we have is our refusal.'

Beside me a man in a well-cut tweed jacket, silvered hair and a moustache, was angrily ripping off the protective cover around one of the newly planted trees and attempting to physically uproot it. An equally well-dressed blonde woman came over to dissuade him. There were instructions to be followed, she said. The next move would be towards the Dáil. Interestingly I heard no Northern accents.

Three rioters with pulled up hoodies and 'kerchiefs

across their faces ran up the middle of the street dragging a large piece of security fencing. All around me teenagers were climbing the new trees and rocking over and back trying to break them.

That's when I realised, I helped to pay for those trees. Whether through central taxation, local charges, commercial rates, we the taxpayers paid for those trees, just like we're paying for the coping stones and the paving stones which were meant to create the new central plaza in O'Connell Street, but which instead were hurled at unfortunate guards and through plate-glass windows. We may yet pay too for the clean-up job and the cases which may be taken against the council for the building material left lying around and used in the riot.

And I remembered the eighties and the republican rioting during the H-Blocks protest period, and how we all felt exiled to the suburbs at weekends, because the city centre, and O'Connell Street in particular, was a no-go area. And I remember thinking, give us back our city. Peaceful protest is one thing. But louts wrapped in tricolours, who claim republican ideals but peddle intolerance, who tear up the city as though it's some sort of gougers' playground, no.

And we don't need a security crackdown and heavy-handed policing. We just need to prepare. More police would have handled the problem. There were only four gardaí standing on O'Connell Bridge when I was there. Had there been a sizeable number of gardaí there, a pincer movement up towards the upper police lines would have trapped most of the rioters and quelled the violence and damage that took place over the next hour and a half.

This is a great city. Stand in O'Connell Street and feel the great wide sweep of it. Stand on O'Connell Bridge and look west up the river in the sunset. Love Ulster, say the Unionist marchers. Yeah, fine.

And Love Dublin, say I.

Housebound

It's now our biggest crop, what we grow best, and it seems we have an insatiable appetite for it. It's taken over gardens and green areas in the city. It's taking over field after field in the countryside. We're abandoning everything else we do to devote all our resources and skills and energy to it. It's Ireland's gold. It's property.

Farmers make more out of selling sites than farm produce. Hotels make more by closing doors to their guests and selling the site. Well-off mothers don't assemble bottom drawers of linen and household goods for their daughters any more. They buy them apartments. Almost the only investment any of us would dream of making now is in houses. It's like every other bubble – the South Sea bubble, the dot com bubble. We've been warned it has to burst, but as long as the price keeps going up we keep buying more. And some day, there'll be a bitter harvest.

Already it's skewing our whole economy. In the late nineties, our industry and services sector were fuelling employment but in recent years anything up to half our jobs growth has been generated by construction and related services. God knows how many public sector jobs have been generated by the huge tax receipts from construction-related stamp duty and VAT.

But isn't this supposed to be an entrepreneurial culture? Isn't that what we boast of, that we're imaginative, great risk-takers? And yet we pour all our money and energy into stolid old bricks and mortar. If you walk into your bank tomorrow with a new invention or a business idea which needs start-up capital, you may not find it easy to get past the front desk. But if you go in to buy a house, no problem. You can get 100% mortgages. Seventy-five to 80% of lending now is to construction-related projects. Can the banks really find no good investment projects in other parts of the economy? Or is it the case that's there more money and less risk in the housing sector – and of course by changing the rules on collateral and deposits, banks can ensure that the demand, the prices, and therefore the profits increase.

Already, companies in the export sector seeking to grow and expand complain that they're finding it difficult to attract and retain workers. Average wages in industry are 600 euros week. But average wages in construction are 750 euros. And for today's bright young managers, the opportunities presented in property are brighter, quicker, flashier. So the skills and ideas which should be building up the productive, exporting sector of the economy, and ensuring long-term prosperity, are being soaked up by the short-term promises of property. Prices and wages are being driven up and our general economic productivity is declining.

And we're building more houses than we need. Up to a quarter of the 80,000 built in 2004 are likely to be unoccupied, bought as holiday houses or investment properties waiting still for a tenant. As long as prices keep rising, that's likely to continue. This is scandalous at a time when we have a massive public housing need, to which the government's response has been pathetic.

The situation has got so out of hand now that there are major social as well as economic imbalances. We have workers with young families living forty and fifty miles from Dublin, because they can't afford the houses built for such families in the affluent Dublin suburbs. Numbers are dropping for the schools and services built for young families in those same suburbs, while schools in the new dormitory towns are overrun and the taxpayer will have to pay for new ones. And what if oil prices go up and the cost of commuting becomes prohibitive? What'll happen to these vast new estates then?

The property boom, which has been allowed to go unchecked, has major consequences, and there are by now no easy answers. The OECD thinks our property is 15% overvalued. But to prick the bubble too suddenly would lead to massive job losses in the construction industry; massive revenue falls; as well as major problems, particularly for those who've recently signed up to big mortgages.

The government could start, however, with a few measures. The Greens have suggested reducing stamp duty for those older people in Dublin's traditional suburbs whose houses are too big for them and who want to trade down. That would encourage the freeing up of houses which were built for young families, and the supply might help ease prices.

A land tax to discourage the holding of development for speculative profit and taxes on such speculative profit is long overdue and indeed many of the ideas in the Kenny Report of the seventies to discourage speculative gain are still worth looking at.

This obsession with property is crushing us, soaking up our energy, our creativity, skewing our society and our economy. We don't do anything else. We don't talk about anything else. We have become a boring housebound people. It's time we got out more.

Home Truths

There's always one sure sign that the ship's about to go down they say – when little furry animals start scuttling off the decks. Beware. The banks are selling their property.

Banks take few risks and up to now property has been the sit-on-it surefire investment. So why did Allied Irish Banks sell part of their Ballsbridge site about eighteen months ago and sell another large tranch to property developer Sean Dunne recently for 200 million euros? Why are Bank of Ireland planning the sale and leaseback of so many of their branches? What do they know that we don't know? Well, they know they need more capital to secure their massive lending. But they also know the market is peaking.

After years of bullish comment about the housing market, a market fuelled by their own readiness to lend massively, the banks are now sounding warning notes. An AIB Group treasury report recently described the Irish housing market as 'a hothouse'. Bank of Ireland has remarked that knowledgeable investors are moving to equities rather than property. Rising interest rates and an over-heated market are finally slowing the juggernaut.

So if the housing boom is at last coming to an end, what are we left with?

Well, the main thing we're left with is a weakening of the concept of home. I've always winced at the way Americans refer to the place they live not as 'our house' but as 'our home'. I thought it was typical American sentimentality. But maybe they're right. In recent years, I've heard people refer to the places they live in as their 'pensions', their 'nest-eggs', 'the best investments they ever made' – but not as their home. We're supposed to think of trading up, or trading down as though a house was something we sloughed off like a snake did its skin, rather than the place with the bump in the lawn where the kids had their paddling pool, or where you could sit and chat on the turn of the stairs where the morning sun poured in – somewhere enriched not by its market value but by our own lives and those of our children, our friends, our neighbours.

We've also seen a social regression, a return to more primitive attitudes. All through the twentieth century, we had progressed to understanding the notion of human capital. We had learned that educating our children as best we could was the best way to enrich and empower them for the world they had to face. We had moved away from the obsession with handing on the farm or the business or the property, and we had begun to appreciate the value of a more enlightened form of enrichment which freed people up, made them independent. That was education.

As a result, most of us in our fifties are better off than our parents. They educated us and left us free to head off independently and make it for ourselves – and maybe help them out as they got older. It was a healthy escape from the tyranny of inherited property. That relationship has changed. Education continues, but it may be that our children's generation will be less free, less well-off than we are because they can't afford rents and they can't afford house prices and they are dependent on us to re-mortgage and give them the deposit for a flat or house. Otherwise, they'll sit at home, resentful thirty-year-olds, waiting for us to drop off. There's a danger that we are becoming the modern Irish version of the ancient parents sitting on the farm while the bachelor children wait for us to die.

And what about the rows that ensue when we have to sell up to provide for old age? After all, there's a direct relationship between the Irish obsession with property and our lack of pensions. Only half of us have pensions and so our houses are our pensions. The potential for family disagreements over property is massive – family property which used to be called home.

Young couples wanting to start a family are elbowed out of the market by investor buyers – how many invest-ment houses have you seen left empty, not even rented, by people who know they'll double in value over a few years? As for those depending on state-provided housing, their neglect by local authorities and by this government has been simply outrageous.

And what about those people who are left commuting sixty miles to work every day because Dublin house prices have made them refugees – what damage has that done to the concept of home? What sense of home life is there in a dormitory estate in outlying counties where children are dropped off to crèches at eight in the morning and where the family meets only late in the evening or at weekends? Commuting has scattered the family and the community. People spend as much time alone in their cars as in their houses. Home is where the car is.

Oh yes, we pay dearly for houses in Ireland – and money is only the half of it.

Lost in Translation

In the hotel and restaurant sector where 21% of workers are non-Irish, language can pose a problem. So to avoid any communications difficulties with customers, one leading Irish hotel insisted the restaurant staff learn the menu off by heart, knowing the exact name of each course and each dish. One evening, an English couple who had arrived late wanted something sweet and they rang downstairs to room service. The Polish waiter on duty dashed into the kitchen, the chef was appealed to, pots and pans flew and after a great flurry, the waiter rolled a trolley into the guests' room, and triumphantly whipped off a silver cover to reveal ... two plates of beautifully fried black and white pudding. They had asked for pudding. They got pudding.

There can be misunderstandings over language, and over culture. Like the Iranian waiter in another hotel, usually totally reliable, who started to disappear at about 6.30 in the evening just when it was beginning to get busy. It was only when they confronted him that they discovered that it was the time of Ramadan, the great Muslim festival, and having fasted and prayed all day he could only eat after sundown. He presumed everybody knew that.

We're all having to learn fast and we're moving into a second chapter in the emigrant story. Until recently, non-Irish workers have worked mostly in the private sector and not the public sector – except of course, for health.

But now, we're beginning to see non-Irish moving into the public sector too. Take Dublin Bus which has fifty-seven different nationalities among its drivers. The sign out at the Broadstone training school says 'welcome' in about thirty languages. Dublin Bus had a recent recruitment drive to meet new EU requirements for the forty-eight-hour week, and they say the majority of those applying were non-Irish. The first group of trainees I spoke to was made up of four Nigerians, an Angolan and an Algerian. They had been in Ireland for between five and seven years. Half of the second group were also Nigerian. Most had suffered discrimination of some sort here, they said, in jobs in supermarkets, warehouses, and restaurants. But Dublin Bus, where average earnings for drivers, after overtime, works out at about 41,000 euros a year, gave them a chance of permanent pensionable employment. They were now unionised, and once they mentioned Dublin Bus, they said, had no problem getting a mortgage. They were buying houses in places like Tallaght, Ballyfermot and in County Louth. Most were married men with children. They were here to stay.

And they matter, because if we have a diverse society, that diversity should be reflected in our services. It hasn't happened yet in the civil service, partly because of the need to have good English – Irish hasn't been a requirement for decades. Outsourcing to agencies means there are lots of non-Irish workers doing security and cleaning work in the public service. However, Michael Coffey of the Federated Union of Government Employees questions whether they are all getting the pay and conditions required by law.

And that brings us to the great battle being fought between employers and unions over protecting pay and conditions, particularly in the private sector, as bitter a clash as we've seen for a decade, and one which puts the question of non-Irish workers right at the very top of our economic and social agenda. Talk to employers and they will tell you that emigrant workers have saved the Irish economy by allowing growth, by acting as a brake on wage increases to keep us competitive, by often working harder and better than their Irish counterparts – but still earning more money than they would at home. Irish unions will say that many immigrants are exploited and that they work harder and longer hours, because they have no home life. 'If you live in Ireland, then you should be paid a wage to live a full life in Ireland,' says Mike Jennings of SIPTU. 'Not enough to live a half life in Ireland and a half life in Latvia.'

What it comes down to is that there is a law which

imposes a minimum wage and basic conditions for all workers in this country. However, employers who don't obey that law know they have a very good chance of getting away with it. Even on the government and the public sector's own contracts, the law is being ignored, as evidenced by the scandal of the Poles working on the refurbishment of the ESB's Moneypoint plant who, it is claimed, were being paid only a third of the legal rate. If the government turns a blind eye to this sort of operation, we will all pay dearly for it down the line.

Right now, we're enjoying the novelty of new faces, new races, new food and culture. A whole new China-town has grown up all along Parnell Street, where the menus and the chatter and bustle in the evening-time could make you feel you're a continent away. A few yards down behind O'Connell Street and you come to the Slavyanskiy Bazar, a Slav grocery bar with newspapers from every East European country and more varieties of sausage and pickle than I knew existed in this world. Walk up Moore Street and flanking the fruit stalls are African hairdressers and boutiques and Afro-Caribbean supermarkets and cute girls peering out from kiosks which sell international telephone cards in every language.

And of course there's a welcome right now because our economy is crying out for foreign workers. Foreign workers use the bus and have contributed substantially to the rise in Dublin Bus passenger numbers over the last six years to about 150 million a year now. Sit on a packed

38 bus heading out to Ballycoolin, Corduff and Damas-town at seven in the morning and you are surrounded by sleepy Poles, Lithuanians, Liberians, Nigerians, Camer-oonians, Spaniards, Russians as well as some Irish. They're heading out to feed the great maw of companies spread throughout the industrial estates in west Dublin of which the best known is IBM – or to staff the crèches and restaurants which service them. Take the same bus back an hour later and you're surrounded by even sleepier people from the same nationalities coming off the night shift. They're here to work. There's plenty of work for them and they're fuelling the furnace of growth.

But what if there's a slow down, what if workers are pitted against one another for scarcer jobs and the twi-light operators know that they can use with impunity imported labour on half-wages? It is the government's job to see that the law is upheld and that there are enough labour inspectors to impose it. So far, the government hasn't done that job and with any economic squeeze there is a danger that we'll go backwards, that a wedge of suspicion and hostility will be driven between Irish and non-Irish workers and that the social consequences down the line will be massive.

It's all too easy to whip up fear. The steadying influ-ence, the solid foundation on which the next phase of our immigrant story is built must be the rule of law. People have to be able to trust the law before they can really start trusting one another.

The Ferns Report

Of course children were slow to talk about it. They didn't have the language. When I was a child, nobody spoke about sex. Nobody explained the facts of life and you knew not to ask. The church and the culture seemed to believe that ignorance equalled innocence. There were body parts whose names were never breathed out loud. Even women who suffered from breast cancer didn't talk about it because you couldn't talk about breasts. The Catholic Church imposed its sternest rules on sexual behaviour and laid a great blanket of silence over the whole subject. A celibate clergy patrolled us all with zeal.

I remember the local curate shining his torch diligently up and down the one and sixpennies in our makeshift town-hall cinema, just in case anyone might steal a kiss. I remember being dressed in a shirtwaister dress on a summer's day, and being warned to put a cardigan on and not to be creating scandal by going up the street 'in my figure'. In plays at my convent school, if we had to play men, we had to wear detachable nun's sleeves peeking below full length coats, because it was immodest for us to wear trousers. When a progressive head nun decided we should wear divided skirts for PE, Reverend Mother worried that they, too, were immodest. But she had a heart attack when she saw the rows of shower cubicles in the new sports pavilion because girls might see one another's naked bodies. I never remember those lovely new showers being used all the time I was at school.

Everything to do with sex was dirty: dirty books, dirty writers, dirty films. Purity was the great virtue. There was an Italian saint called Maria Goretti, whose hair grew long to cover her nakedness when she was sexually attacked, and who died in defence of her virtue. The Church was big on Maria Goretti.

The severest punishments were for sexual sins – women banished from their homes, locked up in Magdalen houses. And I even remember a Catholic bishop in the eighties on radio bemoaning the introduction of the contraception culture, because it meant that sinners didn't pay the price (by which he meant pregnancy) of their sin. Oh yes, you had to pay the price of the sin and sex was the worst sin of all.

And yet, faced with the knowledge that its priests had sexually abused little children, had offended, to use its own language, against all that purity and innocence, the Church was silent. I remember interviewing the late Bishop Larry Ryan of Kildare and Leighlin, a gentle and decent man, ten years ago and I asked him why the bishops, like himself, didn't act more decisively to remove offending priests from all contact with children. Did he not realise the effect sexual abuse had on children? 'It never dawned on anybody that the victim was going to suffer as a result of sexual abuse,' he said. 'One contributing factor may be the fact that the victims didn't say anything.' But wouldn't it be obvious that a heinous crime like this would affect a little child, I asked him. 'It might be. I don't know.' Asked about the Brendan Smith case and the failure, even when his superiors were aware of abuse, to remove him from contact with children, the bishop said: 'I'm not so sure that even the people who recognised he was doing this were aware of the effects it would have on the children. I think the indications are it didn't dawn on people that it would have lifelong effects.'

And this from a church obsessed with sexual sins as the greatest sins of all? This from a church which saw control of its people's sexuality as central to its whole mission? This from a church which insisted that only the celibate, only the purest, can wield its power, preside over its rituals?

There's only one explanation for this callous disregard for its own laity, this readiness to tolerate the worst sexually perverted crimes by its own priests while it rained fire and brimstone on ordinary healthy sex between consenting adults. And that explanation is the belief by an all-male hierarchy that priests are more important than the rest of us; the belief that anything which might damage the power and reputation of the institutional church must be pushed aside; the belief that the Church is more important than God's justice.

So no one was listening to the little children, even if they had been given the words to describe the horrors of what was done to them. They had no words then. We have no words now.

Extract from Olivia O'Leary's
companion volume,
*Politicians and Other
Animals*

Monkey Business

I was listening to Environment Minister Martin Cullen talking about election spending the other day, and it struck me that politicians and their supporters live in a different world from the rest of us, particularly at election times. They tear around, pushing election leaflets at us, but all the time looking over their shoulders at the opposition. Sometimes it feels like you're in the middle of the chimps' tea party at the zoo – noisy, wasteful, where they're much more interested in throwing custard pies at one another than in the effect they're having on the voter.

It's a sort of a mad game. I remember the big trick for one political party in our town was to grab the telegraph pole outside our house and put a large portrait of their leader on it. Then they'd fall around laughing as my mother, who supported the other lot, came out of the house and averted her eyes every time she passed the offending poster.

Nowadays it's a normal part of the campaign that one party spends time pulling down the others' posters. One candidate in Munster is suspected of sending teams out to deface his own posters and win him a sympathy vote. And there's a new wheeze since rules came in that you have to remove all your posters eight days after polling day. Now rival parties take down *your* posters, hide them and put them back up after the eight-day deadline, causing *you* maximum embarrassment and a fine. This is a really nasty one to pull on the Greens.

And that's the least of the chicanery. In one Dublin constituency in 1997, a high-spending candidate went around complimenting the people on their lovely street and their lovely houses. But if they voted for the rival candidate, he pointed out, she would change their area by bringing in thousands and thousands of refugees. Oh yes, she lost.

It's often not the rival party but your own party colleagues that you have to look out for most sharply. The big trick is to say that your party colleague is fine – that you're the one who needs the votes. Famously, in Dublin in the eighties, one candidate put out a leaflet claiming that, to spread the vote, the party wanted people just in that particular part of the constituency to vote Number 1 for him and then Number 2 for his party colleague. The only problem was that that leaflet went out all over the constituency, and the party colleague had to put out a rival set of leaflets to correct it.

Tony Gregory's first Dáil attempt was in Dublin Central in 1981, in the middle of the H-Block hunger-strike campaign. While Gregory had some sympathy with the

H-Block cause, it was a contentious issue and it wasn't part of his election platform. Still, he woke up on polling day to find that overnight the constituency had been plastered with posters saying 'Vote No. 1 Gregory – support the hunger strikers.' The posters were stuck all over shop windows, shop doors – wherever they were going to cause most annoyance to shopkeepers, and they were most plentiful in the middle-class areas where the republican connection was likely to put voters off.

Gregory says he spent the morning fending off outraged shopkeepers and voters. He tried to pull down posters still wet with paste but, by that stage, people had already seen them and left for work – it was too late to undo the damage. He never found out who did it, but he missed the seat by 150 votes.

So this is what they get up to at election times. This is the sort of time-wasting, money-wasting, neighbourhood-defacing chicanery that election money often gets spent on, and now, NOW, Martin Cullen wants to let them spend more money so they can do more of it! As it is, each candidate is allowed at election time to spend €20,000 in a three-seater, 25,000 in a four-seater, and 30,000 in a five-seater. These are big sums of money. One third should well cover the cost of your leaflets and posters – unless you go mad altogether, and some do. There are presidential-style campaigns run in Dublin, particularly on the northside, with massive full-length portraits of the candidate more redolent of Saddam Hussein's Iraq than a small western democracy.

Martin, however, has hinted he wants to raise the limits. 'It's not the limits that matter,' says Martin, 'but transparency about spending.'

So they can spend millions but as long as we know about it, that's all right then, is it? More money for posters that deface the place? More money for election handouts that end up in the dustbin, or the gutter? More money to give an electoral advantage to those parties who can raise it, over those parties and candidates who either can't or, on principle, won't? More money to create an unholy alliance between corrupt business and corruptible politicians, the sort of corruption the tribunals were set up to investigate?

Martin Cullen is a bright minister with some very good ideas. This, I'm afraid, ain't one of them.

The Face on the Poster

A couple of years ago, when Bertie Ahern and Celia Larkin were together, Ruairí Quinn defended the relationship. Ireland had moved on, he said. Indeed, who knew whether we mightn't one day have a gay or a lesbian Taoiseach?

It was an act of political chivalry which didn't do him any harm. The phone calls rolled in and one man in particular insisted on speaking to him direct. 'Are you Ruairí Quinn?' he demanded. Quinn said he was. 'Remember what you said about us having a gay or lesbian Taoiseach?' asked the man. 'Well, I'll tell you one thing. We'll never have a baldy Taoiseach!'

Quinn tells the story with a certain ruefulness. He's been long enough in the business of politics to know the importance of image – or to know, as Hillary Clinton once declared, that *hair really matters*.

In fact, during the last general election, looking at the range of aspiring baldy Taoisigh and hairy Taoisigh postered up across the country like a spreading measles rash, it was interesting to see how the hair issue was addressed. Bertie Ahern had plenty. Quinn's head was edged off the top of his poster emphasising beard rather than baldness. Michael Noonan's portrait cleverly edged him sideways into the shade – as a result a fetching shadow clothed the top of his head. The late and much-loved Charles Mitchell of RTÉ knew all about that trick. In the old black-and-white days of television, Charles would use a black marker to draw a line across the top of his naked pate to give an impression of hair while read-ing the news. Did we take him more seriously as a result? Well, he believed we did.

But back to the poster – there's always a subliminal message. Bertie's portrait in shirtsleeves meant he was hardworking, a man of the people, a trick learned per-haps from the successful Eoghan Harris election portrait of then Democratic Left leader Proinsias de Rossa in shirt-sleeves, swinging his jacket over his shoulder.

Then there was the nice 1987 election poster of outgo-ing Taoiseach Garret FitzGerald working at his desk in the glow of a green library lamp. It was trying to tell us that this was a man who cared and worked for us, maybe even at night when we're fast asleep.

His family loved that poster – they have it hanging up at home – but of course it didn't work. Maybe there were people who thought we'd all be safer if Garret went to bed. Maybe there were unfortunate echoes of that great Stalinist lie about the lights being on all night in the Kremlin because Uncle Joe was up late worrying about the people.

Indeed, there was something a bit Stalinist about many of the candidates' shiny new colour portraits in the 2002 election. Mary Harney, who takes a good photograph anyway, had been airbrushed almost to the point of obliteration. Michael McDowell – well, maybe there's not a lot they can do with Michael McDowell. Eoin Ryan looked about five and a half and Gay Mitchell was accused of using his Holy Communion photograph.

'I had me picture taken only a few weeks ago!' protested Gay, driving around his constituency and fretting that too many of his posters had been blown away by the wind. Eric Byrne, who waited a few days before putting his up, was weathering better. 'But we are re-postering,' said Gay firmly.

Now if ever there was a man who didn't need to aid voter recognition in his own constituency, it's Gay Mitchell. He can't finish a sentence without people interrupting to say hello, or to beep their horns as they pass by.

Gay needed more posters? Rubbish! And that's exactly what election posters become – rubbish in your street and mine, along with the glossy leaflets through the door, the bags and hats handed out in supermarkets, all the electoral detritus which hits the bin.

Except that all this stuff costs money. When politicians were explaining in recent years why they took money from business people, they had a handy catch-all excuse – they needed it for electoral purposes – in other words for all the election gunge that litters our homes and our streets.

Imagine then an election world with no posters and leaflets, where politicians had to make direct contact with the voters and answer their questions; a simpler, cleaner world where contributions for electoral purposes could no longer be used a cover for corruption?

Imagine a world in which we might even be able to elect a baldy Taoiseach.

Politicians and Other Animals is available from www.obrien.ie
and all good bookshops.
ISBN: 978-0-86278-880-3